IN THE SUICIDE MOUNTAINS

Illustrated by Joe Servello

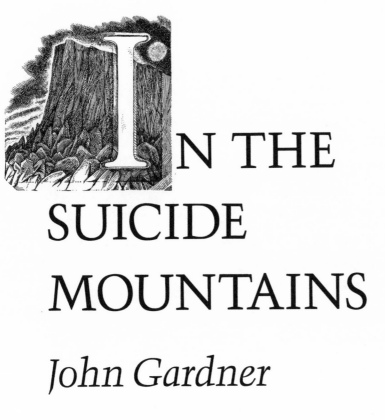

IN THE SUICIDE MOUNTAINS

John Gardner

Houghton Mifflin Company   Boston

Copyright © 1977 by Boskydell Artists, Ltd.

Library of Congress Cataloging in Publication Data

Gardner, John Champlin, date
  In the suicide mountains.

  Reprint of the 1st ed. published by Knopf, New York.
  I. Servello, Joe. II. Title.
[PZ4.G23117In 1980] [PS3557.A712] 813'.54 80–12156
ISBN 0–395–29468–1 (pbk.)

Printed in the United States of America

M 10 9 8 7 6 5 4 3 2 1

The abbot's tales and the baby's tales are adapted from
traditional Russian fairy tales as collected by Aleksandr
Afanas'ev, translated by Norbert Guterman.

Reprinted by arrangement with Alfred A. Knopf, Inc.
Houghton Mifflin Company paperback edition 1980.

To Liz

IN THE SUICIDE MOUNTAINS

n a certain kingdom, in a certain land, there lived a dwarf who had an evil reputation, for he was humpbacked and ugly, with teeth like a saw's and skin like a mushroom's, and his legs were crooked and his eyebrows were hairy, as were his nostrils and ears, and the eyes that peered out from the shadow of those eyebrows were as mottled and devoid of vitality as two dead mackerels. It was rumored that he knew everything there was to know about black magic, and that by saying certain spells through his long, bushy beard he could cause an ordinary house to turn around so that its back door faced the street. It was said that when he liked he could turn himself into a flowery valley or a housefly, and that whenever he was angry, or even merely bored, he

caused women to have warts and the village priest to get roaring drunk on tap water.

It was all lies and fictions, for the dwarf, whose name was Chudu the Goat's Son (for his mother had been a goat and his father a magic fish), had all his life scrupulously avoided using magic for improper ends, or even, as a general rule, for proper ends. Even when his heart was swollen with rage, as it frequently was—and as it always was when he heard the villagers' slanderous talk—he kept himself tightly reined in and merely counted to ten, or to a hundred, or to a thousand, or to whatever proved necessary. Walking down the street, keeping close to the curb, where he could easily step off into the gutter if some villager should desire to pass, he would listen to their slanders and be so furious that his eyes, lifeless no longer, would bulge and fill with boiling hot tears. Visiting the grocery store not far from where he lived, buying his supper of turnips and buttermilk and sometimes a can of tobacco for his pipe, he would hear (for his hearing was unusually acute) some foul-faced old woman mumble hoarsely into the ear of the creature at her side, "Take care! There goes Chudu the Goat's Son! Don't look him in the eye!"

Chudu the Goat's Son would suck in air as if he intended to blow the whole grocery store down—as he could have if he'd wanted—and his mushroom-white face would go dark as a brick, but he would contain himself, would take his groceries to the counter and pay for them, would even smile, as best he could, at the grocer, and would carry them home to his shack at the edge of the village. His heart, all the way, would go *wham, wham, wham!*, but only when the door of his shack was closed and the shades were all drawn and the grocery sack was set carefully on the table, would the dwarf's pent-up violence erupt. "Confound, confound, con*found* them!" he would yell in his reedy goat's voice, stomping so hard he made the floorboards bend, and sometimes he would tear off his hat and hurl it to the rug and stomp on it, hard, with both feet, and stomp on it again and again until the hat cried out, "Mercy!"

He'd done nothing to harm anyone in all his days, though he'd been tempted. He was not to blame, despite village gossip, for the wine's going sour in the Church of St. Laslas the Levitator, or for the year's poor cabbage crop (on the contrary it was thanks to certain spells of his that the crop had done as well as it had, that year), nor was Chudu the Goat's Son responsible for the steady increase in outrages in the Suicide Mountains (that was all the work of the six-fingered man, the man no jail in the world could hold), or for the tiler's old mother's falling tail-over-tincup down the coalchute. But it was useless to protest his innocence, useless to show by word or deed the essential benevolence, self-control, and unmagical orderliness of his nature. The dwarf had been chosen as the village scapegoat, and nothing he could do would change it.

This he had proved beyond a shadow of a doubt. He'd left baskets of food on the doorsteps of the poor and had hid himself in some nearby bushes to see the expressions of the people when they came out and saw. When they came and discovered what the baskets contained, their doughy faces would grow radiant as moons, and they would throw up their hands and say, "God be praised! Our luck has changed at last! It must be that Chudu the Goat's Son has died, or perhaps he's found somebody new to persecute. No doubt we'll soon be as well off as everyone else!"

The Goat's Son was hardly surprised by their reaction, though it grieved him and also, though he hid it, made him hopping mad. One day, to forestall their mistake, he left a large white card on the top of the basket, which said in bold black print, "From Chudu the Goat's Son." When the people he'd given it to saw the sign, they screwed up their eyes and pursed their lips and looked cautiously to left and right; then they got a long stick of the sort one might use to knock a wasp's nest down, and they caught the handle of the basket with the stick and carefully, tremblingly carried the whole basket of fruit and bread and delicacies to the trash pile and burned it. Chudu the Goat's Son tore off his hat and stomped on it ferociously—but quietly, taking care, as usual, that no one should see him, for the last thing he wanted was to support people's foolish prejudice that that was his real nature.

The world rolled on, and things went from bad to worse for the Goat's Son, and he began to feel depressed. He kept more and more to himself, getting through his days as best he might by reading the dictionary or trying out various new recipes for turnips or walking up into the mountains to sit by the railroad trestle, watching the great, square trains go over, thinking what horrible things he might do if he were the creature the villagers imagined him to be.

Sitting by the trestle, watching the trains come lumbering across with their warm and yellow lighted windows, the coaches crowded with half-sleeping travelers—now and then a bespectacled conductor leaning over to peer into the darkness and discover how far they'd gotten, figuring how early or late they were by now and whether or not he'd be at home and in bed by midnight—the dwarf would suddenly be overwhelmed by a feeling of irrational, jealous rage that positively awed him, so foreign was it (he told himself) to his real nature,

or at any rate to the nature he had adopted, the nature he intended to live by. He could imagine the train exploding into a thousand fiery sparks, the long, high trestle bridge parting with a terrible *crrraaack* at the center, then horribly sagging, tumbling slowly, slowly into the chasm as a boulder sinks into a lake or one falls in one's dreams. So vivid was the picture that the dwarf would sometimes imagine for a moment that he'd actually done it—made the train explode—not willfully but by accident, his knowledge and beliefs momentarily captive to some terrible, subhuman grotesquery at the center of his being. Sweat would pop out; his whole body would tremble. But the bridge, he would realize the next instant, was intact, the train still rumbling toward safety beyond the gorge.

"Perhaps," thought the dwarf one wintry night when this had just happened to him, and with extraordinary force, "Perhaps I am going mad." As if the thought had jerked him up, as a string jerks a puppet, he bounded to his feet and began banging his fists together, pacing back and forth on the high, moonlit ledge where he'd been sitting. "Woe is me," he said aloud. "Am I in control or not?" He suddenly stopped stock-still and began tugging at his ice-crusted beard with both hands. His eyes widened, his mouth opened, and his expression became fixed. Then abruptly he brought out, his thick lips quivering, "One has serious reason to doubt one is as sane as one had hoped."

The red swinging lanterns on the tail of the train were just vanishing now around the bend of the mountain. The dwarf breathed more deeply, calming himself. The night air was freezing. In the bottom of the chasm there was fog, faintly lighted by the snow.

He began shaking his head, slowly and thoughtfully, like a country doctor who has encountered a case beyond his learning. "Who can say who might have been a passenger on that train?" he asked himself. After a minute he added, as if scolding, "Perhaps the king himself, or the queen, or the crown prince, Christopher the Sullen. Who can say how close I came to snuffing out their lives, snipping the thread of their destiny without even knowing it, mindlessly waving my scissors about like some reckless, drunken tailor?" The dwarf was moved by this poetic image—horrified, in fact—and again he saw in his mind's eye the coaches of the train falling slowly, gracefully, gradually separating, yellow lights gradually sinking in the abyss. It was all, in the dwarf's mind, as silent as the end of the universe, just a few distant screams. "In potential, at least," the Goat's Son thought, "I'm as dangerous as the nastiest of the villagers maintain. What am I to do?" It crossed his mind that when a dog went mad, or an ox or a rooster, one chopped off its head. Chudu the Goat's Son gave a shudder, turned on his heel, threw a quick look over his shoulder, and started for home.

All that night, though he struggled against it, the dwarf was troubled—both awake and asleep—by the awful idea of suicide. His dreams, which came thick and fast as snowflakes, were unspeakably frightening and left his teeth chattering. In the morning, determined to get the better of himself, he snapped his eyes wide open abruptly, as if the lids were on springs, gritted his teeth, threw his crooked legs over the side of his small and splintery wooden bed, and began whistling as if cheerfully, even before he had his nightshirt off and his clothes on. He whistled as he fixed himself breakfast, whistled more cheerfully still as he put on his overcoat and mittens, and whistled as he stepped onto the drifted porch with his snow-shovel. The world was blinding white, beautiful and crisp, but on the road in front of his house there were two old women in heavy black overcoats and heavy black shawls, looking up in alarm at him. They ducked their heads and began to run, fearing his black magic, and the dwarf stopped whistling and began shaking all over, for he'd been tempted, indeed, to use it on them, had been tempted to snap them into two fat sows, or two hot pies on a bakery cart. There could be no escaping it, he saw now: he would have to kill himself. For what the priests said was true: "Life follows art; words can grow teeth and eat tigers." He went back inside where it was warm, put the shovel in the corner, and sat down to think.

Speedily a tale is spun; with much less speed a deed is done. The following morning, which was the day he'd decided on, the dwarf changed his mind. The day after that he changed it back again, but then once again he reconsidered, and then again reconsidered, and so the dwarf continued, vacillating between life and death, now resolving once and for all to be done with it, now reflecting that, after all, one's luck might change, nobody knows what tomorrow may bring, and so on and so forth, endlessly, drearily torturing himself, until finally spring came and the dwarf discovered that, for no clear reason, the matter had in some way settled itself without his help: he was going, so to speak, to make the jump.

He wrote a sad but businesslike note and laid it on his kitchen table, one corner tacked down by the sugar bowl, then on second thought decided, no, he would not leave a note, it was a petty and vindictive thing to do; since no one loved him, no one would miss him—in all probability, no one in the village would even know he was gone until the shack fell in, and crooked and ugly as it might be, it was solidly built. He crumpled up the paper and threw it in the stove, then stood pulling at his beard, trying to think what he'd neglected; but there was nothing, he owed nobody. At last he sighed and stepped out on the porch and locked the door behind him and prepared to start his journey. His plan was simple, though indefinite. He would walk until he found the perfect place—in the Suicide Mountains there were many good places—and then quickly, before he had time to reconsider, he would do it. Chudu the Goat's Son nodded, trying to convince himself that this was indeed what he intended. A muscle in his cheek twitched, causing him to appear to wink like a conspirator. His winter of soul-searching had made him a wreck.

Nevertheless, he put his left foot down, and then his right foot, and soon he was in the mountains. The trees were so thick with birds that their music filled the road like fallen yellow apples and he could barely pass. But he remembered his purpose and continued to put his left foot down and then his right foot, and after a time he became aware that on the road ahead of him, walking all alone, there was a woman. She was tall and slender and had hair like yellow straw, and every now and then she would pause for a moment and lean against a tree to sigh. "How curious," thought the dwarf. Once, in a fit of what seemed sudden fury, the woman struck the tree with the sides of both fists, and the blows had such force that the treetrunk broke, exactly where she'd hit it, and the top sagged over, withering. "Stranger and stranger," thought the dwarf to himself. He hurried closer, studying the woman to see if he'd be wise to overtake her.

hen Chudu the Goat's Son came even with the woman who'd been walking ahead of him, he found that she was young and beautiful, each feature more beautiful than the last. But what struck him most forcibly was the contradiction between what he'd seen with his own eyes, when she'd broken a beech tree with her two bare hands, and her appearance now—her complete transformation to flimsy elegance. She appeared to be a princess. Her wrists, though not small, seemed barely to hold the weight of her hands; her throat—blue-white and encircled not by jewels, as one might have expected, but instead by a simple peasant's chain—seemed barely to sustain the weight of her head; and her waist, as dainty in relation to the rest as the waist of an hourglass,

seemed a structure too delicate by far to support her bosom and broad, sloping shoulders.

Despite this general feebleness, or limpness, or, to put it in a kinder light, airy grace, the young woman walked with long, quick strides, so that the dwarf, to keep up with her, had to trot and even, occasionally, break into a run. She was, like everyone else, much taller than he, and like everyone else she disliked him, or gave him that impression. She never turned her face or acknowledged his existence by word or glance, but strode on, chin lifted, lips pouting, her hair streaming behind her like a golden flag.

She was not in the least alarmed by him, it seemed, and Chudu the Goat's Son was puzzled by this. His appearance, he knew by experience, struck fear into the heart of the boldest desperado, yet this wisp of a maiden was as indifferent to his ugliness as an ostrich would be to an oyster. This made the dwarf so curious he began to forget his natural timidity—his hatred of getting his feelings hurt. He began, indeed, to forget himself entirely. He pursed his lips and beat his fists together and fell into such a serious fit of concentration that his head tipped sideways of its own volition and little by little his eyes crossed. Then, suddenly having reached his decision, the dwarf churned his crooked legs faster than before, moving out in front of her, where she'd find it more difficult to pretend not to see him, and abruptly stopped short, whirled himself around, grandly swept his hat off and bowed from the waist, so low that his forehead bumped the roadway. As he brought himself erect again, he saw the most puzzling thing of all—just barely glimpsed it from the corner of his eye as she came barging past: though she was gliding like the wind,

on strides as powerful as an antelope's, she tipped him a timid little feminine smile, whispered some inaudible, timid little greeting, and took a limp, quick swipe past her nose with an invisible fan. *So pleased to meet you*, her lips seemed to mouth. But her eyes—and this greatly startled him—her eyes were furious with hostility, and tears sprayed out of the corners like drops of winter rain.

The dwarf stood stock-still, still with his hat off, watching her hurry up the mountain, around the sharp bend, and out of sight, and then he went and sat on a stump and got his pipe out and stoked it. He pondered and pondered, puffing smoke into the trees, trying to unscramble the riddle of the hurrying maiden: but not even the comforting tobacco could help him, and so at last, with great dignity shaking his head and brushing the ashes from his long black beard, he stood up, absently put the pipe in his vest, turned himself into a sparrow, and hurried to catch up with her.

When he caught sight of her, the maiden was standing by an ancient, towering oak, with her left foot drawn back and the muscles of both legs bunched, preparing to deliver the tree such a kick as would tear it from its footing. In his disguise as a sparrow, the dwarf flew down to her, screeching as if in terror in his piping voice, "Oh yes, destroy our home! Do whatever you please with us! What are poor hapless little sparrows to you—you who have the powers of a dragon? We look forward, at best, to but a year or so of life, but you, you live a thousand, unless I miss my guess, so you can easily afford to hold life cheap!"

At this, to his astonishment, the maiden put her left foot on the ground beside her right and began to weep and cry more heart-brokenly than before, like a poor spanked schoolgirl.

"Little do you know," the maiden brought out at last, "how far I am from holding life cheap! You must forgive me for threatening to harm your home. I only meant to vent my rage at the cruelty of my fate." And now again she was sobbing.

"It must be a terrible fate indeed," said the sparrow, ruffling up his neck feathers, still pretending to be angry, "—it must be a terrible fate indeed that you should feel yourself justified in taking it out on harmless bystanders! But tell us your story, for many's the grief for which God is relief, and there's one or two for which *I* am."

"Very well, I'll tell you," said the maiden, "but take my word for it, there's no relief in sight, and I tell you my troubles only because I owe you, I suppose, an explanation." With these words, her blue eyes both weeping and flashing, the maiden sat down on the green, mossy bank beside the road, and the dwarf disguised as a sparrow settled comfortably on a branch.

he girl was a blacksmith's daughter by the name of Armida. Her childhood had been happy, for her mother was a great, fierce, chortling woman who might have been a blacksmith herself if matters had gone otherwise and she'd been born a boy. But she took her misfortune in good spirit, as she always took everything in life, and pleased herself mostly with woman's work, cooking and sewing and tending to the cow, which she sometimes carried to the field, for pure sport, on her shoulder. Armida's father was a gentle, simple-hearted man who never cared a tittle for what people thought, as long as he got his dinner and his wife was good to him. He paid no attention—in those days anyway—if neighbors scoffed at the lack of decorum and convention in his house,

for what was it to him? Their horses still needed shoeing, didn't they, whether or not his wife, for pure pleasure, chopped down timber? They still needed chains made, and plowshares shaped, though his wife in her spare time carved tombstones. His household got increasingly out of hand, at least from his neighbors' point of view, but the father grinned placidly, sipped hot, flat ale from his dented tin cup, and continued to let things slide. Thus it befell that when Armida was a baby, she got the habit of puttering in the glow of the forge, shoveling in coal or fashioning door-bolts or bending heavy iron in the company of her father, instead of helping her mother in the kitchen where she might have learned woman's work.

"You're a fool, Otto Ott," the neighbors said, upbraiding her father. "That daughter of yours will grow up headstrong and powerful as an ox in May, and not a man in this world will ever hazard his life by marrying her."

"God's will be done," said her father with a grin, for Armida was just nine, and it seemed to him no problem.

"Perhaps the neighbors are right, Otto," her mother sometimes said, for though she was a merry, boisterous person, she had a deep, uncommon mind, and understood things as nobody else did.

But Armida's father, who always enjoyed it when her mother opposed him, however casually, would guffaw and feint and get the drop on Armida's mother and would pin her arm tight-as-a-clam behind her back, and the two of them would wrestle, laughing and puffing and kicking up dirt by the wheelbarrow-load, until her mother sucked in breath and broke her father's hold and slammed him against the barn's oak wall and knocked the last gasp of wind out of him. Then they'd laugh and laugh.

One night when Armida and her father came in from bending iron bars, they found her mother's two feet sticking straight up like stumps under the wellhouse roof, and her head under the water, and to their horror and terrible sorrow she was dead. The neighbors, though perhaps they meant no harm, could not help feeling that the fault was Armida's father's. Had Armida been working in the kitchen, as she should have been, the tragedy, they said, would not have happened.

Her father's heart was broken, and his self-confidence as well, and so, after he'd buried Armida's mother—in a grave he'd dug out of solid rock and covered with a foot-thick iron door—he gave in, to the last detail, to his neighbors' whims. He married a widow who had distant relatives at the king's palace, and into her hands he put the training and grooming of Armida.

Alas that Armida had not died in that well with her mother!

The step-mother, who had a daughter of her own who happened to be exactly Armida's age (and whose name was Clarella), was wonderfully gentle and kind to Armida when her father was near; but whenever his back was turned, she was mean as a snake. "Hopeless, *hopeless!*" she would hiss, with a look of spiteful glee, for Armida could do nothing right. She made her read books to see what heroines are like and told her to study her step-sister. She showed her paintings and read her poems and gave her exercises.

In one of the exercises which the step-mother used, trying to make Armida "an aristocrat," she said, "instead of a staggering, rolling-eyed horse," it was necessary to carry a book on one's head. Armida, though pretty as a picture, heaven knows, was so strong that the weight of a book was like the weight of a feather in her hair, so that for the life of her she couldn't tell where the book was and thus couldn't balance it. Strange to say, out of love for her father—and because she shared, deep down, his remorseful feeling that the family had gone wrong, and that the neighbors were right—Armida was eager to please the step-mother, cruel as she might be, and learn, like a dutiful student, all her step-mother had to teach. Though she had liked her old life and loved her true mother, she couldn't help feeling that what the step-mother said was true: Armida ought to be, like Clarella and the heroines in poems and stories—to say nothing of the ladies at tournaments and fairs, or at railroad stations—flimsy and graceful, helpless and fluttery when gentlemen were near, and whenever conversation turned serious, silly as a duck.

For this reason Armida worked night and day, part of the time reading, part of the time trying to balance books on her head and make her posture aristocratic—all to no avail. But Armida, like her mother before her, was gifted with an uncommonly good mind, and so she thought at last of a stratagem: when everyone was asleep she unfastened the stovepipe from the wall and put the stove on her head, and in this way she learned to walk head-erect, with the grace and light-footedness of a kitten. She learned, soon after, how to hide the fact that she had bones in her arms, and after that—by imitation of her step-sister, and by long hours of diligence—she learned to talk stupidly, as if nothing, even simple addition, could penetrate her skull.

In hardly more time than it takes to tell, Armida became—to her step-mother's horror, to say nothing of the horror of her jealous step-sister—the most sought-after eligible young lady in the Suicide Mountains. Her father was neither pleased nor displeased, so far as one could tell; he merely drank his ale, fondling his dented tin cup as if it were his one last possession, and the more Armida watched him —furtively peeking out past the flowered chintz curtains on the kitchen window while she scrubbed the pots and pans—the more fearful she became in her heart. Then one night, by accident or not, her father fell into the forge which he'd fanned with his bellows to its hottest, and all that was left in the morning was the soles of his shoes.

Poor Armida! If her life had been terrible before, it was now ten times more terrible. When suitors came to visit, her cruel step-mother and cruel step-sister would listen critically at the door, and whenever she made some mistake, they would cackle like two witches. Nevertheless, the suitors kept coming until the whole house reeked with their flowers and was piled like a granary with their greeting cards and favors.

"Disgusting!" said her step-mother, picking up a love locket, newly delivered, between her long, pale, lumpy fingers.

"Well hello! It's the walking honey pot," said her step-sister, and gave a quick jerk to Armida's yellow hair.

Poor Armida could well understand their scorn, for however she might hide it, her intelligence grew keener every day. She was a living lie, that was the heart of it. It was that, she could see, that lured those admirers to her door like ants: the aura of mystery that, in spite of her best intentions, she gave off like a scent of sachet. Little did they dream, those innumerable admirers, how simple, how unspeakably vulgar, was that mystery at the core: behind her elegant, filagreed facade, her studied femininity, those shoddily stolen little tactics of her step-sister's—the fluttering lashes, the shy gazelle eyes—she was manlike, firm of flank as a farmer. They wrote her sonnets and graceful, silly sestets, gave her thimbles and real-silver sealing-wax sets, invited her to ride in their canoes by the summer's moonlight. What would they have thought if she were suddenly to reveal that beneath the pink ribbons of her lacy dress she had the muscles of a drafthorse, and under her burst of yellow hair the acumen of a banker? Yet it was so.

"Ah, mother, father, how unhappy I am," she would sometimes whisper, lying in bed beside her sleeping step-sister, and a tear would trickle down her cheek. The more she was loved, the more she hated herself, and also the more she hated everyone around her. It began to be the case that, however soft her gestures, however unintelligible her murmured words, her blue eyes had moments of sparking like the eyes of an anarchist. Though admirers kept coming—she had never a free minute—she could see that they were jumpy, suspicious as cows on the train to the slaughterhouse, in the presence of her choked-in violence. The number of her admirers increased as the frightening sense of mystery increased, and she grew still more unhappy. Moreover, she could not help feeling sometimes, rightly or wrongly, that on rare occasions—but now increasingly often—the admirer sitting primly in the plush chair across from her, speaking lightly, amusingly (with slightly trembling fingers) of the bloodthirsty exploits of the "six-fingered man" (of whom she'd never heard and in whose bloodthirsty exploits she felt no slightest curiosity or interest)—or the admirer standing heavy-footed as a mule, pretending to listen as she played for him *Für Elise*—was glancing furtively past her in the direction of her step-sister. How much happier her admirers would have been with Clarella, had they only the sense to see it—Clarella whose femininity had been nurtured from her earliest childhood, so that by now it was as real, as whole and translucently unmysterious as a china dish or, say, a potato sprout.

The world rolled on, and things went from bad to worse for Armida, and she began to despair. A tragic realization had come to her by now: She hated her admirers for being fooled by her sham; and she hated and envied her step-sister Clarella, for whom the sham was second nature, as it would never be for poor Armida. She hated, in a word, everything. Lying in the wooden bed, irritably listening to her step-sister's snoring, Armida began to dream up schemes. Perhaps she would travel to some distant village and "cross over," as they say—put on the trousers and jacket and heavy leather apron of a blacksmith, and start up a blacksmith's shop. But the thought at once sent cold shivers up her back. There'd been a time when the idea might have appealed to her, but the memory of her former, farmhorse ways was repulsive to her now. She thought then perhaps she would run off to Russia and become a bear tamer, with gleaming boots and a whip and fur hat—feminine but fierce, barbaric but not downright masculine. And maybe in the middle of a performance, a great, black bear would grow unexpectedly rebellious, would lash at her throat in his lightning-fast rage . . .

Tears brimmed up in Armida's eyes and she found herself thinking about suicide.

It might have ended there, for in the morning she felt better; but the following afternoon, young Gnoff the Miller's Son, her step-sister's only suitor, brought Armida a rosewood box and Clarella nothing. After supper she heard her step-mother and step-sister whispering, and on tiptoe she went over to listen, bending down beside the door.

"Mother," said her step-sister, sobbing into her hankie, "I've had all I can stand. Armida imitates me day and night—she's like a walking mirror—and now she's stolen from me my one and only suitor!"

"Hush, dear, Mama knows," the wicked step-mother said. "Buck up, my child. Do as I say and your troubles will all be over." Then, whispering still more softly, covering her mouth with her two milky hands (peeking through the keyhole Armida saw it all), the step-mother said, "Tonight when Armida's fast asleep, you push her clear over to the edge of the bed, and then stay back out of the way, and I'll come and chop her head off."

Armida listened in horror to these words, then hurried back to scrub the pots and pans.

That night she lay awake at the edge of the bed until she heard her step-sister's snoring, and then she got over on the side against the wall and pushed Clarella to the edge and lay perfectly still, waiting. Sure enough, in came her wicked step-mother carrying an ax. She groped about in the dark with her hand until she found Clarella's ear, and she felt for where the neck was, and then down she came with all her might with the ax and so chopped her own daughter's head off. Then she groped back to the stairs and went down to her bed.

"What a sinner I am," thought Armida. It was as if she'd awakened from a witch's spell and could suddenly see things plainly. She

sat bolt upright, then crawled out of the bed before the blood could get all over her, and she hunted till she found an old birthday candle, and with trembling hands lit it, and as she held it up to look into the staring, once lovely gray eyes of Clarella she thought, bursting into tears, "I might as well have murdered my poor step-sister myself! What's become of me? I must be mad!"

And now in a rush all the nice things Clarella had ever done for her came leaping—once, for instance, Clarella had shared her sandwich with Armida, after someone had stolen Armida's lunch. Armida stepped away from the body, sickened, the back of one pale hand pressed against her forehead, tears streaming down her nose and cheeks. As she was stepping back another step, and after that another, she caught a glimpse of her frail white reflection in the mirror, and the image made her skin crawl. It seemed not the image of herself at all, but the image of feeble, nigh-transparent Clarella, all gossamer shimmies and expiring fibrillations, all rolled-up eyes and drooping sighs, but with manly shoulders and powerful thighs.

"Horrible!" she thought again. "I've become neither of us—nothing!"

That moment the door opened at the bottom of the stairs, and Armida's step-mother called up sweetly, "Is that you, dear?"

"Yes, Mama," Armida called down in Clarella's voice. But Armida's step-mother wasn't fooled for one minute and came flying up the stairs like a hawk after a chicken, and she was waving the ax and rolling her eyes around, and would have killed Armida for sure this time, had not Clarella done Armida one last favor. The old woman in her haste stepped on Clarella's severed head, which rolled so that her feet went flying out from under her, and the ax went flying from the old woman's fingers and came smack down on her own forehead, which it split in two pieces like a pumpkin.

"Horrible and more horrible!" thought Armida, and wrung her fingers. By morning she felt so guilty she made it definite: she would go up in the mountains, and the first good place she saw, she would kill herself.

"And that," said Armida, rising with a sigh from the bank where she'd been sitting, "is the reason I'm up here, traveling through the mountains, full of remorse and, sometimes, rage."

"But my dear *girl*," cried the sparrow. Every feather stood on end and he was fluttering and fussing, distressed by Armida's story and alarmed by her intention. He cocked his head, winked one black eye, and suddenly he was Chudu the Goat's Son, leathery cheeks twitching.

y dear girl, you mustn't do it!" said Chudu the Goat's Son, twitching and winking like a madman. Now, too late, he realized he'd made a mistake in turning back into himself. Armida was staring at him in righteous indignation, her fine eyebrows arched, her chin drawn inward and quivering, and to make matters worse her whole body was in confusion, torn between kicking him, as a farmer would kick a horse, and fainting dead away, eyes rolled upward, like a maiden shocked.

"You tricked me!" exclaimed Armida, her soft voice helpless, and she resolved the conflict toward the maidenly, and wept. "You've made me tell secrets I'd never told anyone!" Her hands, like orphans, clung tightly to one another, and her face, drained of blood, was as white as snow. "Oh, I wish I were dead!" she moaned, so sincerely that his heart almost stopped in its tracks. And now she wept in earnest.

The dwarf was so upset, so angry at himself and eager to atone, somehow be made use of—even if she should send him to point at pheasants, like a dog—that he tore off his hat without thinking and threw it on the ground and stomped on it. "Please, master, *please!*" cried the hat, but he went right on stomping it.

When he'd vented his emotion, or some of it, he plucked up the hat again and put it on his head—where it sat trembling and whimpering, swearing to itself—and he said: "Armida, let me tell you I understand how you feel. No one knows better than I what a terrible thing it is to—"

But he saw she wasn't listening; she'd taken advantage of his tantrum to collect herself. Still weeping and sniffling and brushing tears from her cheeks, but shaking her yellow hair out, her breast heaving less now, she'd walked up onto the road and was prepared to stride on. He gave a little jump when he saw what she was doing, and hurried to catch up with her.

"I too have a double identity of sorts, Armida," said the Goat's Son, awkwardly running along beside her now, pitifully looking up at her, the top of his head not even level with her waist. There was nobody else in the world to whom he'd have confessed his secret. He threw a quick look around the dark, slanting woods to see if anyone had heard him. There were a couple of round, brown bears bumping shoulders, and a wide-racked deer standing absolutely still, and on every hand there were twittering songbirds, but so far as he could tell they were all authentic, not shape-shifters. He pressed on fervently:

"As a matter of fact I came up here into the mountains myself, just like you, to kill myself." He stretched out his arms, skipping sideways, imploring her to listen, and awaited her reaction.

"Beat it," she said angrily—not with cruel hostility but like an older sister, as if the troubles she experienced were beyond his ken—beyond, ha!, the emotional understanding of Chudu the Goat's Son, who was two hundred and seven years old! Yet he saw himself accepting it: he would burble, grovel, do handsprings; he, Chudu, was her captive, he'd be anything she pleased.

Perhaps it was Armida's intuition of that—the abject adoration of the ugly little dwarf with the great, black shark-mouth, the short arms extended in miserable entreaty, the crooked legs hurrying like the blades of a butterchurn—that made Armida once more burst out crying; for love is no small imposition, especially unrequited love; and though his experience was limited, even after two hundred years and more, since he was seldom even liked, Chudu the Goat's Son understood pretty well all the ironies that enclosed her like the ribwork of a cage: here stood *he* for whose deformed and spiky love she had no faintest desire, and back in her village sat those foolish suitors. She had no one she respected who could love her for herself. It grieved and enraged him that he, Chudu, should be the cause of such distress—that his horrible adoration should awaken in her heart an idea of the kind of adoration she desired and, in all probability, would never never find in this whole vast universe.

She was rubbing the knuckles of both fists into her eyes, crying and striding on.

"What I told you is true," he said. He danced out in front of her and ran backward. "I'm not tricking you, Armida. I'm not lying to you. I really did come here to commit suicide. I'm going to do it, too." His cheeks twitched and jittered like a rabbit's, and he hammered his square right fist into his square left palm.

Deep in her own grief, she didn't even trouble to look down at him with distaste. "I'm not surprised," she said.

Before he could answer, his left foot tripped over his right, and he fell. She went by him. He scrambled to his feet.

They'd come to a shoulderlike crest on the mountain, a respite. Beyond, the road dipped downward for a stone's throw, then lifted again, much more steeply than before. Behind them lay the valley dotted with white villages, churchspires sticking toward the sky like little pins; ahead of them the mountaintop, vanishing into haze, ascended like God's gray jaw. The trees all around them were luminous and wide-beamed and curiously still, as if grown against a plumbline, and the golden beams of light that settled slanting through the leaves, dappling the high-crowned curving road, gavotted like young swallows in Armida's yellow hair. The beauty made Chudu the Goat's Son heartsick. Like a baby, like a billygoat, he bawled out after her, forsaken and forlorn, standing there splay-foot, clench-fisted, humpbacked, drowning in woe: *"Armida, don't do it! Don't kill yourself!"* Chudu the Goat's Son's heart went light, plummeting like an elevator when the cable has snapped, and he began, in great whoops, to cry.

Armida slowed her pace. After a long moment she stopped completely, then veered around to face him. Her eyes were still wet, but she was in control now. "It's *my* life," she said. "Go away, dwarf. It's none of your business."

Chudu the Goat's Son, however, was not in control by any means. He cried harder and harder, as he hadn't cried since childhood, two hundred years ago, and his anger at crying like a baby, augering his fists into his eyes as if to blind himself, made him stamp first one foot then the other then both at once. "It *is* my business," he bawled. "It's very much my business!"

His eyes were too filled with tears for him to see that she was studying him, startled at last. But her voice was remote, withdrawn—she was thinking of herself, not of him—when she said, "I don't care. I just don't care."

She was about to draw away from him. He snatched at her loose sleeve and held it.

"Think of the people who love you, Armida! Think of how they'll feel!"

His eyes were blurry with tears but he caught, even so, her angry smile and knew what she was thinking. All those suitors.

"Please," she said, and now her princesslike feebleness seemed unfeigned, her limpness of neckbone, wrist, and elbow: for sorrow of heart she could hardly have picked up a pencil. "I need to get it over with."

"No!" he said, ferocious, and with sudden bold madness jumped his hold from her airy and insubstantial sleeve to her wrist, to which he clung like a lobster.

As if he'd caused it, there came a thunder of hooves.

ike an angel of vengeance the knight came galloping, he and his horse leaning far, far over as they boomed around the curve, and then righting again as they came plunging down the straightaway, the horse with his head down, ears laid back, the front hooves slamming down from level with his nose. Chudu the Goat's Son was too terrified to run, too terrified to think, though he was usually calm in emergencies. It was guilt, perhaps: clinging to Armida's lovely wrist, he was in the wrong, no doubt of it, though his motives were pure; but whatever the cause was, the dwarf stood rooted there, knees knocking, hair straight up, his eyes enormous, and his instinct for self-preservation somehow jammed, or momentarily went crazy, so that without being actually

aware of it he was shape-shifting wildly, twelve creatures per second, now an owl, now a lion, now a woodcock, now a yellow Jersey cow, now a sheep, now a mouse. The lance came straight at him, and the horse and the knight; and the desperate shape-shifting had no effect whatever except that the knight jerked his head once, as if trying to fix his eyesight or shake a pod from his ear. When they were practically on top of him, the lance aiming straight at his adamsapple, his whole life hurriedly passing in re-run (and strange to say, he found himself paying close attention in spite of himself, fascinated: "My goodness! There's Aunt Urtha!" he thought, transported, for he'd been fond of her, and, "There's Uncle Ah-ba-ak the Camel!" so that Chudu the Goat's Son might not even have noticed if, that instant, he'd been killed)—Armida cried out, with the powerful voice of a boxing official, "No, wait!" The horse put the brakes on, and horse and knight, with a terrible noise, came skidding at Chudu sideways.

Armida gave his arm a jerk, snatching him clear, and the horse slammed past him into a tree. The knight went rolling, over and over and over, like an armadillo, and though he'd parted from the horse he apparently didn't know it, for he was still bellowing, in a tragic, hopeless-sounding voice, "Whoa Boy! Whoa!" Finally he came to rest and, after a moment, sat up and shook his head to clear it and tipped up his visor and looked around.

Chudu was still trembling, though not in his dwarf's shape; he was in the shape of a small pink-eyed pig, which Armida held gently, firmly, under her arm. Limp and princesslike as she appeared, and comfortable as it was between her arm and breast, she stood like a hundred-year-old elm.

Now the knight got unsteadily to his feet and, after testing his

legs, walked, staggering a little, to where his horse lay. It was uncon-
scious. He got down on his knees and listened to the horse's heart,
then opened a sort of saddlebag-like thing and got out a waterskin,
which he opened and emptied onto his horse's face. The horse shook
its head and came to. Then, glancing up at Armida and the pig, the
knight remembered himself and said, in an official voice that seemed
studied and somehow unnatural for him, "What seems to be the trouble here?"

Armida pointed to the horse's foot. "That horse of yours has got
a shoe loose," she said.

"Hmm," the knight said, and bent over to look. Then alarm
came over his face, and he went to the saddlebag-like thing again and
dived his iron-gloved hand into it and brought out, to the surprise of
Armida and the pig, a violin.

"Christ!" he said, and it sounded much more like a prayer than
like swearing, "I thought for sure I'd broken it."

"You," the pig said, tipping its head, "—*you* are a violin player?"

But the knight said nothing. He was looking for something and
couldn't find it. "It must've fallen out," he said. "Darn!" He began
walking down the road he'd come galloping up before, retracing his
horse's steps.

"What are you looking for?" Armida said. "Can I help you?"

"The bow," he said. "It's a wooden thing, with horsetail on it.
It's about this long"—he held his gauntlets apart in front of him, separated by about two and a half feet.

"I know what a violin bow is," said Armida.

"Sorry," the knight said.

"What's-your-name," she said to the pig, "find the man his bow."

Chudu the Goat's Son came to his senses now, blushing at his foolish wish to stay there between her arm and her breast all year. He changed back into a dwarf and then, on second thought, into an eagle and flew off to find the bow. He found it nearly three miles back, picked it up—carefully not touching the strings with his beak—and returned it to its owner.

By now the horse was standing up, and Armida was holding his right back leg up, bracing it professionally, hammering in the shoe-nails with a rock.

"Be careful," the knight said, "he's a kicker."

"He won't kick *me*," Armida said.

The horse laid back his ears and looked at her and decided he better not.

The knight watched her with respect. So did Chudu the Goat's Son. The horse was as big as a house, and Chudu the Goat's Son, for one, wouldn't have touched that hoof for a hundred million zloti.

"You're damn good at that," the knight said when Armida put the horse's foot down.

Armida merely smiled and looked shy and silly in the elegant way she'd learned from her step-sister. The knight blushed, suddenly shy himself. "Perhaps we should introduce ourselves," he mumbled. "My name's—" He paused, for his eyes had accidentally met Armida's and it seemed he was about to have a heart attack. He looked at the violin bow in his right-hand gauntlet and said, addressing the ground, "My name's Christopher the Sullen."

Instantly—quicker than an ax could fall—both Armida and Chudu the Goat's Son dropped to their knees, for Christopher the Sullen was the kingdom's crown prince.

"Don't do that," yelled Christopher the Sullen. "Please! I *hate* that."

Instantly they got up.

But the day was ruined. His personality had changed completely, and even a chicken could have understood how it was that he'd gotten his name.

e'd come up into the mountains, the prince said morosely, because the king had ordered him to. (The three of them were traveling up the road again now, the prince and Chudu the Goat's Son walking—Chudu scrambling to keep up, sometimes falling—Armida riding on the big white horse. He had a black nose with pink spots on it. "What's your horse's name?" Armida had asked the prince, fluttering her lashes. "I don't know," the prince said. "They told me, but I forgot. I call him Boy.") Christopher the Sullen had no liking for quests, and no liking for tournaments or fights or politics, all of which, as crown prince, he was forced to make his business. He was the unhappiest man in the world. Also, he said—giving a little tug at the horse's bridle, because every time the road went under low-hanging branches the horse

would reach his head up for a mouthful of leaves—he, Prince Christopher, wasn't what you could call *good* at quests or fighting or politics, and he made no bones about it.

"I was sickly, as a child," he said gloomily, looking off into the woods—they were dark now, toward the middle—"and I never really did get my strength back. But that's the least of it." He pursed his lips, looking now at the ground a few feet ahead of him, for the confession, Chudu the Goat's Son saw, was embarrassing for him to make. It was a mark of his despair that he made it anyway, as if nothing at all mattered one jot. "That's the least of it," he said again, and nodded. "The sickness apparently affected my mind. A prince is supposed to be clever. Quick-witted. Ha." He glanced over at Chudu, then back at the ground again. "I'm doltish, that's the truth. Sometimes I forget to tie my shoes."

"But you're good at heart," Armida said encouragingly.

"Not really," said the prince. "Take horses, for instance. I'm not so stupid I haven't noticed how 'real men,' as they say, feel about horses—the way they pat them lovingly, you know, when they dismount, and always think of their horses' needs first on long journeys. Read stories of knightly adventure, it's all there." He glanced at his horse as if to see if he was listening and decided, fool that he was, that horses don't understand. "I hate horses," he said fiercely. "My favorite way to travel is on a train."

Chudu the Goat's Son thought of his nights by the railroad trestle and shuddered.

"Oh, there are *some* things I like about horses," Prince Christopher corrected himself—for one of his faults, as his father was always telling him (since it was a serious disadvantage in government work), was that Christopher the Sullen was abnormally fussy about truth. "I like the smell, for instance. Somebody should bottle it. But as for the rest . . ." He glanced at the horse's nose. The horse's black lips parted, trying to give Christopher the Sullen a nip. The prince jerked his hand away. Armida, unbeknownst to the prince—her face still empty of intelligence as a plate—patted the horse to calm him and distract his mind.

They walked on for a time in silence. Prince Christopher, who had his steel helmet off now, had long, raven-black, shiny hair, as soft and beautiful and well-cared-for as a woman's. It flowed halfway down his back and had a wonderful smell; it took all Armida's concentration to resist reaching forward and touching it, sniffing it, pressing it to her lips. His dark, handsome eyes were also womanish, and so were his gestures. When he waved his free left hand, gesticulating, he reminded her of an Indian princess. And she noticed this too: When lost in thought he had a funny way of pursing his lips as if preparing for a kiss. She blushed.

"I should never have *been* a prince," he said. "It's all some absurd mistake. All I really care about is playing the violin. I'm really good at that. And also, occasionally, I like to read books. I like books quite a lot, actually, though people say it's sissy." He added in haste, "Not science books or history books." He glanced at them. A blush rose up his neck but he wouldn't stop confessing. "I like poems and stories. I do. I wish the whole world was run by poems and stories. 'Why not?' I say. People laugh. Poems are for girls, they say. I say 'Pish!'"

"Personally, I hate poetry," Armida said, and then looked nonplussed, for she'd been trying not to let any thoughts slip out.

"I don't believe it," the prince said simply and impolitely. He looked up at her, eyes brightening. "You want to hear a poem?"

Armida pursed her lips, glanced at Chudu the Goat's Son, and said nothing. The Goat's Son chuckled grimly. He did like poetry, but only poetry about caves.

Prince Christopher's face became more animated, and his walk, in some curious way, took on conviction, though he wasn't walking faster. "It's about a juggler," he said. "A juggler who's a magician. It's a poem I wrote myself."

Prince Christopher the Sullen was striding now, striking his legs out like an Irish dancer, his right hand still holding the bridle of the horse, his left hand pressed against his chest so that he could feel the fremitus as he spoke. The sun was slanting into the woods almost sideways—it would soon be dark—but the prince, declaiming his poem, was like cock-robin early in the morning. "The Juggler and the Baron's Daughter," he began, "by Prince Christopher the Sullen."

It went:

> *Draw in near!*
> *Draw in near!*
> *Draw in near to*
> *The jolly old juggler!*
>
> There once did live
> A rich baron's daughter,
> And she'd have no man
> That for her love had sought her,
>> So nice she was.

And she'd have no man
That's made of bone and meat
But if he had a mouth of gold
To kiss her on the seat,
          So *grand* she was.

And so the jolly juggler learnt,
Lying on the heath,
And at this pretty lady's words,
Forsooth he grit his teeth,
          So *cross* he was.

He juggled him a mighty steed
Out of a horse's bone,
A saddle and a bridle too,
And sat himself thereon,
          So *sly* he was.

He pricked and pranced that mighty steed
Before the lady's gate:
She swore he was an angel
Come there for her sake.
          (A dunce she was.)

He pricked and pranced that mighty steed
Before the lady's bower:
She swore he was an angel
Come from Heaven's Tower.
          A prancer he was.

Then four and twenty knights
Led him through the hall;
Mean-while, as many squires
Led his horse to stall
                    And bade him eat.

The squires did give him oats,
The squires did give him hay,
Bút he was a mean one
And turned his head away.
                    He wouldn't eat.

Then day began to pass
And night begun to come;
Up to her bed was brought
This gentle wo-mun.
                    The juggler too.

Then night began to pass
And day begun to spring,
And all the birds around the bower
Begun at once to sing.
                    (The cuckoo too!)

"Where are you, my perty maids,
That you come not me to?
The jolly windows of my bower
I pray that you undo,
                    That I may see.

"For I have here inside my arms
A duke or elst an earl."
But when she looked upon the man,
He was a blear-eyed churl!
            "Alas!" cried she.

She bore the juggler up a hill
And meant to hang him high:
He juggled him into a meal poke,
And dust fell in her eye.
            Beguiled she was!

Christ and Our Lady
And sweet Saint John
Send to every haughty maid
Such another one!
            Amen.

When he'd finished, the prince looked up at Armida and boyishly grinned. "What do you think?"

"Strange rhymes," she said, and smiled shyly. She glanced down at the horse, which was blinking merry tears out of his eyes and chuckling.

Prince Christopher looked at the horse in surprise and found he was beginning to feel friendly toward him. "You like that?" he said. The horse nodded and chuckled harder. Prince Christopher mused. As had often happened, in his experience, poetry had mysteriously reclaimed the day. "You want to hear another one?" he asked.

Armida leaned forward in the saddle and batted her eyelashes. "Maybe later," she said.

Though he'd intended to at the start—if only from curiosity about what kind of poetry a prince might write—Chudu the Goat's Son had not paid particular attention to the poem, or anyway the last few stanzas of it, for he was thinking, with gradually increasing excitement, that perhaps Prince Christopher the Sullen might be the answer to his prayers. When poetry put the prince in a better disposition than was, apparently, normal for him, his antics had a tendency to distract Armida; and like a bolt out of the blue it had occurred to the Goat's Son that such a tendency, pushed to an extreme, might in the end lead Armida to forsake her intention of committing suicide. With an eye to finding out how long the prince might be expected to remain with them, the Goat's Son said now—with what seemed to Armida, the prince, and the horse an uncivil abruptness—"So your father, you say, ordered you here on a quest."

It was a stupid thing, he saw at once, to have said. The prince suddenly became more dejected than ever.

"It's filiacide," he groaned, and in the failing light the Goat's Son was just able to make out that large tears were falling from the prince's beautiful dark eyes. In his misery—as if the whole burden of the world had dropped on him—the prince seemed not so much to walk as to stagger. He threw his left hand up in a dramatic gesture, the right one still holding the bridle. "I have to slay an outlaw," he said and heaved a sigh. "The notorious six-fingered man."

"*I've* heard of *him!*" Armida said, then stopped herself and in haste made her face shy and foolish.

"Everyone," said the prince irritably, "has heard of the six-fingered man. Master of disguises, heart of a dragon, the man no jail in the world can hold—" He walked on a few steps, shaking his head, the tears still falling. "I haven't got a prayer. He'll kill me like a rabbit! What match is a mere poet and violinist for an experienced murderer?"

"Perhaps when the time comes," Chudu began, but he let it trail off. Prince Christopher was right; he had no chance. In his mind he saw Prince Christopher lying on a heath with an arrow through his heart, Armida kneeling beside him in a long black dress, inconsolably weeping. He, Chudu, would wear his top-hat.

"Well," Armida said, cheeks flushed with distress, "you'll simply have to do your best."

Christopher the Sullen laughed. It was a terrible thing to hear and made the night—or so it seemed—grow abruptly darker. "That's what everybody says. 'You'll have to do your best.' I don't agree. Not one bit. It's stupid! And undignified! There I'll be, rattling my mighty lance and yelling *'En garde, vile villain!'* and there *he'll* be, smiling, sitting with his legs crossed, fiddling with his pen-knife—" The shame of it made Prince Christopher cover his eyes with his arm. "I won't do it," he moaned. "I *can't!* I'd rather be hanged on a gybbit high!"

"What," asked Armida, lowering her lashes, "is a gybbit high?"

The prince took his arm from in front of his eyes and thought about it. "I'm not sure," he said at last.

Chudu the Goat's Son pushed his hands into his pockets and pursed his lips. After they'd walked a little further, Chudu the dwarf taking three steps for every one of theirs, Chudu asked, gloomily fearing he could guess the answer, "Well then, Prince Christopher, what do you intend to do?"

"I'm going to kill myself," said the prince. "I've made up my mind."

Chudu the Goat's Son nodded. "I thought so," he said.

Armida gasped and peered through the darkness at the prince as if she might not have heard correctly. "You mustn't!" she said. "Oh, you *can't!*" She pressed her hand to her bosom.

"I can do anything I please," snapped the prince, "and I intend to."

Armida fell silent, abashed at having had to be yelled at. *"I love him,"* she thought, heart full of anguish, and was astonished at herself. Tears began coursing down her cheeks, but no one saw, for it was now dark as pitch. Ahead of them, at the top of the mountain, flimmering at the very edge of Suicide Leap, there were lights. It was the Ancient Monastery.

"ome in, my children," said the abbot.

In the hazy dimness of the hallway behind him, where bats flew silently from beam to beam, and holy brothers hurried quietly, like owls, about their evening chores, there were numerous sick people lying in straw on the flagstone floors, with their relatives sitting or standing nearby, saying prayers, and their neighbors peeking in through low doors. The saintly abbot was famous far and near for his ability to heal the sick by miraculous means; also for his gentleness and wisdom. His powers were legendary; there were songs about it. From far and wide people came to him for help, and though the abbot couldn't understand himself his miraculous power, he said, for he was no better than other men, at least in his own eyes, and perfect neither in love nor in faith, nevertheless he would admit himself (this he would say with his glowing, bald head tipped sideways, quizzical) that he seemed in some way to exert a beneficent influence, or else his legend did; he seemed, without consciously trying, merely joking and praying, in fact, to elevate the courage and faith of the sufferer so that "occasionally," as he said (but he was absurdly modest), a cure did indeed take place. He gave the credit all to God.

"Come in, come in," said the abbot again, bowing in a way that seemed faintly oriental, his baggy eyes beaming, his great bald dome gleaming, his ancient miracle-working hands buried deep in the folds of his floor-length black cassock, and he backed away—lightly, almost dancingly, in fact, though he was a man in his seventies—to give them room.

Armida entered first, then Chudu the Goat's Son, scraping his cap off with one hand and looking around him in alarm and angry distrust, then Prince Christopher the Sullen, who threw one last gloomy look in the direction of the horse being led to his stable, which was somewhere around back, then stepped in and closed the door behind him.

"You're just in time for supper," said the gentle old man, and his smile was so warm, so absolutely simple and pure and personally affectionate, that even Chudu the Goat's Son was inclined to partly trust him.

"Thank you, father," said Armida, and for some reason curtsied.

Prince Christopher the Sullen said, "Let us introduce ourselves. This is Armida, and this is—" He glanced down at Chudu the Goat's

Son, but the dwarf flicked his eyes away. It was against his policy to tell anyone his name. Prince Christopher looked puzzled but retired behind a sad smile and did not press. "This is Armida's dwarf," he said, "and I am—Christopher."

The abbot lit up. "Ah ha! Prince Christopher the Sullen! Exactly! I *thought* I recognized that incomparable, grieving face! I've seen you, light of my life, in visions." He brought this out with such perfect simplicity that no one even noticed that the claim might have seemed, on some other man's lips, preposterous. He leaned forward, toward the prince. "How's your poor father?"

"Much better lately, thank you," said Prince Christopher. He'd forgotten that his father had been unwell.

"God bless him," said the abbot, beatifically smiling, and his eyes went unfocused for an instant, as if he was looking at something far, far distant, quite possibly the Throne of God. "Well!" he said then, "this *is* an honor! Yes yes! Exactly! *Now* we're on the track!—But I forget myself, you're starving!" He nodded down the hallway, past the sufferers in the straw, the watchful relatives and neighbors, toward an archway. "You go right through there, my loves—right through there, exactly!—and the brothers will provide you with fresh clothing and food and anything you need. I'll be in in a minute. I have to—" He smiled and looked floorward, his shoulders briefly rising in a meek, apologetic shrug.

Chudu the Goat's Son said, head tipped back, staring straight up at him with ferocious and unabashedly skeptical eyes, eyes close together and empty and black as shotgun barrels: "You mean you're going to heal these sick people?"

"Well, *try* anyway, with God's help," said the abbot with a laugh.

"Goodness," said Armida, forgetting to look dim-witted, "is it possible that a person might watch?"

"God bless you, my child, for your interest! Certainly you may watch!" He turned his smile toward the prince. "Would you care to watch too?—And you too, of course, my friend." He bent to smile at Chudu.

"I'd be fascinated," said Prince Christopher sadly. The Goat's Son said nothing. He looked more skeptical than ever, and offended, as if someone had insulted his intelligence.

"Fine!" said the old man. "Fine and dandy!" He nodded in the direction of some chairs along the hallway wall. They were wide and comfortable, once-expensive chairs, overstuffed and leather covered, the leather now sewn and patched in innumerable places. The prince, Armida, and the dwarf sat down, and the abbot, with a nod that suggested that he'd be only a moment, went over to the sufferers and their sad-faced families. To a boy who lay rolling his eyes and drooling, snapping at the empty air with his teeth, and occasionally jerking his hands and feet, the abbot said cheerfully, "Well well, my son! What seems to be our trouble this evening?" The boy went on biting and jerking as before. His mother, who was lean and hollow cheeked, her skin gray as ashes, her eyes much too large, raised her hands imploringly and shook them. "It come over him sudden," she said.

"Mmm," said the abbot, and creakily got down on his knees, first one, then the other. Beyond him, holy brothers scuttled back and forth, not even glancing in his direction. He smiled and winked at the boy. "You believe in God, my friend?"

"*Larble,*" said the boy and rolled one eye.

"Good," the abbot said, nodding and smiling with satisfaction. With only his fingertips poking out of his sleeves, he began to pray.

Strange to tell, as the abbot prayed, not only the boy but also the two cripples sitting closest to the boy began to glow all over with an indescribable light. The jerking and twitching of the boy's limbs grew less noticeable, then ceased altogether; he stopped biting at the air, and his eyes no longer rolled. Right next to him, the first cripple's corkscrewed leg began to straighten itself, the foot turning around and around shoe and all until it was exactly as it should be. The cripple bent over to stare in surprise, then yelped and tossed up his hands, wildly joyful, and leaped to his feet and did a tap-dance. The cripple beside him, who had one leg nine inches shorter than the other, watched the dance with interest, then got a startled look and abruptly stuck both legs straight out. Lo and behold, before his very eyes the short leg was growing, about half an inch a second, and soon he was exactly like anyone else. "It's a miracle!" he cried, and leaping up, danced a little jig. The boy who had been twitching and jerking was now smiling from ear to ear, tears of joy on his cheeks. He seized the abbot's knees and began kissing the hem of the abbot's cassock for gratitude, his poor mother screaming and clapping. "Larble," cried the boy. "Larble! Larble!"

So it went. The abbot cured one after another until there was no one left to cure. Then, gently smiling, the abbot came over to where the three friends sat watching and invited them to go in with him to supper.

When they had eaten their fill in the huge, dim room with its long plain tables, the abbot all the while sitting over in the gloomiest corner of the room with his back to the others, for that was one of his penances, he said, and also he'd always been ashamed, he confessed, of the dreadful way he ate, for he could never, try as he might, keep from talking with his mouth full—the abbot led them to a pair of rooms where the prince could get out of his knightly armor into more comfortable clothes, and the dwarf and Armida could find garments that made them look like nobility. After that the abbot led them to a large, stone-walled chamber where the holy brothers had prepared a roaring fire and set out for them brandy and brandy snifters. The abbot declined, with a little headshake, to take brandy. It was sufficient for his happiness to sit gently watching them, smiling and smiling like a fond old grandfather, his hands in the folds of his cassock.

"Well now," the abbot said, "*tell* us about yourselves!"

Armida and the Goat's Son immediately told him everything, opening their hearts as they might have done to God himself. "I've come up the mountain to kill myself," said Armida, and tears filled her eyes.

"And why is that, my dear?" asked the abbot with great interest.

She told him her secret, how she was not at all what she seemed but, God help her, mannish—complex and quick of mind and as strong as a gorilla.

"Ah!" said the abbot.

"I too came here to kill myself, originally," said Chudu the

Goat's Son, bleating it really, for pity of himself. "Try as I may I can never persuade anyone that deep down I'm a civilized, decent sort of dwarf, fit to be an alderman—and indeed, perhaps I'm not. Who knows?"

" 'Originally,' you say?" the abbot softly prodded.

The dwarf glanced over at Armida in confusion. He would bite off his tongue before he'd shame her by speaking of his love. But the abbot, it seemed, was a man who missed nothing.

"Yes, I see," he said, gazing thoughtfully at Armida. "That's grave, very grave. And you, Prince Christopher?" He tipped his head to look above his spectacles at the prince.

"That's why I've come too," said Prince Christopher the Sullen. He was standing by the abbot's mantel, staring moodily into his glass. "I don't care to go into it except to say I'm, as they say, a misfit. I'm a prince by birth, but by inclination I'm an artist. I hide it, naturally, and I admit I'm deeply ashamed of it—"

"You paint?" asked the abbot, sitting forward in his chair.

"I'm a violinist. Also, in a small way a poet."

"Marvellous!" cried the abbot. "You must play for us a little before you leave. I absolutely insist! And you must recite some of your verses!"

"My," said Armida, "I didn't realize how *late* it is."

The abbot laughed aloud. "Something tells me our Armida has been 'overexposed,' so to speak, to poetry." He winked slyly at the prince. "Never mind," he said, "no one can hate poetry indefinitely. It's like trying to think ill of Christmas."

Then some thought occurred to him that made him frown and

purse his lips. He asked, delicately brushing past the slightly awkward word, "This 'suicide' business: you're not planning to do it tonight, I trust?"

"Actually," Armida began, wringing her hands . . .

"No no, really!" the abbot insisted. "Not tonight, I beg you! Keep me company awhile. You know how it is, way up here on the mountain. Besides, I want to tell you a story."

"A story?" the prince echoed, raising one eyebrow but carefully not looking at the abbot for fear of seeming over-eager.

The Abbot's First Tale

T hings are not always what they seem," said the abbot, and tipped his head and smiled. "The sly man digs down through illusion; he picks up a nugget and cries, reading it: 'Ah ha! No man does anything for another man except for personal gain!', and on the back: 'The witch was an innocent child once; the good man, a witch.' Poor fool! The nugget itself is an illusion, and all the nuggets he stands on (so triumphant!) with his spade. They will suck him to the hall of the accursèd king and we will hear nothing more of him.

"In a certain kingdom, in a certain land, there lived a rich merchant who had a beautiful five-year-old daughter by the name of Anastasya. The merchant's name was Marco the Rich, and one thing he could not abide, among many, was beggars. Whenever they came begging at his window he would shake his fist and order his servants to drive them away and loose the dogs upon them.

"One day two gray-headed old men came begging at his window. Anastasya, who was familiar with her father's ways, wept for pity of the two old men and began to implore her father: 'Dear father, for my sake at least let them shelter in the cattle shed.' The father consented and ordered the beggars to be shown there.

"When everyone in the house was asleep, Anastasya rose up and went to the cattle shed, where she climbed up into the loft to watch the beggars. When the time came for morning prayers, the candle beneath the ikon came alight by itself, the old men rose up, took priestly vestments out of their bags, put them on, and began their service. An angel of God came flying through the window and said, 'In such and such a village, a son is born to such and such a peasant. What shall his name be, and what shall be his fortune?' One of the old men said, 'I give him the name of Vasily the Luckless, and I hereby present him with all the wealth of Marco the Rich, in whose cattle shed we are spending the night.' All this Anastasya heard. Now that it was daybreak, the old men made ready to leave the cattle shed. Anastasya went to her father and told him everything she had seen and heard.

"The father decided to see if a babe had indeed been born in such and such village. He had his carriage harnessed, went straight to the priest of the village, and asked him, 'Was a babe born in your village on such and such a day?' 'Yes, a babe was born to our poorest peasant. I christened him "Vasily" and surnamed him "the Luck-

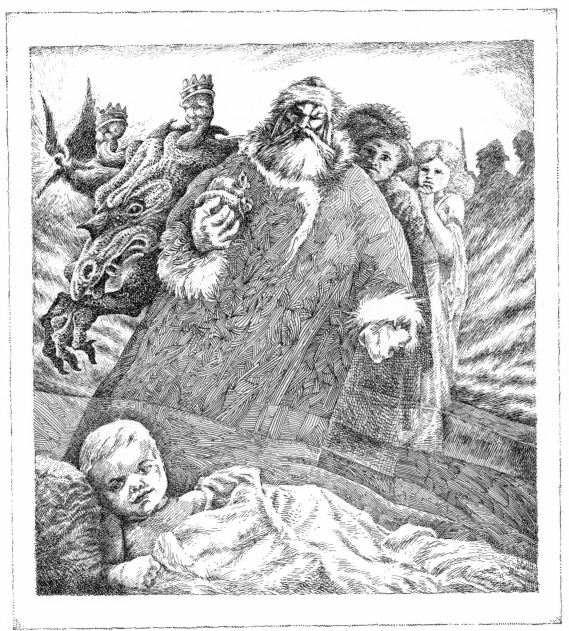

less," but I have not yet baptized him because no one will stand as godfather to such a poor man's child.' Marco offered to stand as godfather, asked the priest's wife to be godmother, and bade them prepare a rich feast. The little boy was brought to the church and baptized, and everyone feasted and sang to his heart's content.

"One day passed and then another, and on the third day Marco the Rich summoned the poor peasant, spoke to him kindly, and said, 'Friend, you are a poor man, you will never be able to bring up your son. Give him to me, then, and I will help him to rise in the world, and I will give you a thousand rubles.' The poor man thought and thought and at last consented. Marco gave him the thousand rubles, took the child, wrapped him in fox furs, put him on the seat of his carriage, and drove away. It was winter. When they had driven several miles, Marco bade his coachman stop, handed him the godchild, and said: 'Take him by the legs and hurl him into the ravine.' The coachman did as he was ordered and hurled the child into a deep ravine. 'Now, Vasily,' said Marco, 'take my wealth if you can!' And he drove home.

"The following day, some merchants came driving down this same road. They were carrying twelve thousand rubles they owed Marco the Rich. When they came near the ravine they heard the wailing of a child, and they stopped, listened, and sent a servant to see what it could be. The servant went down into the ravine and beheld a soft green meadow, and in the middle of the meadow a child sat, playing with flowers and whimpering. The servant told all this to his master, who went to the ravine himself, took the child, wrapped him in a fur coat, returned to his carriage, and drove on. The merchants came to Marco the Rich, who asked them where they'd found the child. 'In a meadow at the bottom of a ravine,' said the merchants, and Marco guessed at once that it was Vasily the Luckless, his own godchild. He took the boy in his arms, dandled him for a time, then gave him to his daughter, saying, 'Take this boy, my daughter, and see to his comfort.'

"Then he plied the merchants with all kinds of drink and asked them to let him keep the child, seeing he'd grown so fond of it. The merchants at first refused, but when Marco told them that he would cancel their debt, they consented and left. Anastasya was so overjoyed that she immediately found a cradle, hung curtains around it, and began to tend to the babe, never leaving him by night or day. One day went by, then another. On the third day Marco came home when Anastasya was asleep, took the child, put him into a barrel, tarred it, and threw it into the harbor.

"The world rolled on, and the barrel sailed one week and then another, till finally it floated up against the bank of a monastery. A monk happened to be fetching water. He heard the wailing of a child, and when he looked about him, saw the barrel. He immediately took a boat, caught up the barrel, broke it open, and found the child. He brought the babe to his abbot. The abbot decided he would name the child 'Vasily,' and he gave it the surname 'the Luckless.' Vasily the Luckless lived in the monastery for sixteen years and learned how to read and write. The abbot loved him and made him his sacristan.

"Now it came to pass that Marco the Rich was traveling to a foreign kingdom to collect some debts that were owed him, and on his way he stopped at this same monastery. He was received as befits a rich man. The abbot ordered the sacristan to go to the church. He went, lighted the candles, and read and sang. Marco the Rich asked the abbot: 'Has this young man been with you long?' The abbot told him how the boy had been found in a barrel, and when. Marco reckoned the time and realized that the sacristan was his godchild. He said: 'If I had an intelligent young man like your sacristan, I would appoint him chief clerk and put him in charge of all my treasure. My friend, you must give him to me.' For a long time the abbot made excuses. Finally, Marco offered him twenty-five thousand rubles for the benefit of his monastery. The abbot consulted the brothers, and after long deliberation they consented to part with Vasily the Luckless.

"Marco sent Vasily home and gave him a letter to his wife. The letter read: 'Wife, when you receive this letter, take its bearer to our soap works, and when you pass near the great boiling cauldron, push him in. Do not fail to do this, or I shall punish you severely, for this youth has evil designs on me and, if he survives, will be my ruin.' Vasily took the letter and went on his way. He met an old man who said, 'Where are you bound, Vasily the Luckless?' Vasily said: 'To the house of Marco the Rich, with a letter to his wife.' 'Show me this letter,' said the old man. Vasily took it out and gave it to the old man, who broke the seal and asked Vasily to read it. Vasily read it and burst into tears. 'What have I done to this man,' he said, 'that he should send me to my death?' The old man said: 'Do not grieve, my child. God will not forsake you.' Then he breathed on the letter and the seal resumed its former shape. 'Go,' said the old man, 'and deliver the letter to the wife of Marco the Rich.'

"Vasily came to the house of Marco the Rich and gave the letter to his wife. She read it, pondered deeply, then called her daughter Anastasya and read Marco's letter to her. This is what the letter now said: 'Wife, one day after you receive this letter, marry Anastasya to the bearer. Do this without fail, otherwise you shall answer to me.' The next day Vasily was dressed in rich garments, shown to Anastasya, and she found him to her liking. So they were married.

"One day the wife of Marco the Rich was told that her husband had arrived in port, and accompanied by her son-in-law and daughter she went to meet him. Marco looked at his son-in-law, fell into a rage, and said to his wife: 'How dared you wed our daughter to this man?' 'By your command,' answered she. Marco asked to see his letter, read it, and found that it was written in his hand.

"Marco lived with his son-in-law for one month, a second, and a third. One day he summoned the young man before him and said to him, 'Take this letter beyond thrice nine lands, to the thrice tenth kingdom, to my friend King Dragon. Collect from him twelve years' rent for the palace he has built on my land, and find out what has happened to twelve of my ships that have not been seen these three years. Set out on your way tomorrow morning.' Vasily took the letter, went to his wife, and told her what Marco had commanded. Anastasya wept bitterly but dared not ask her father to change his mind.

"Early next morning Vasily prayed to God, took some biscuits in his knapsack, and set out. He walked the road for a long time or a short time, a long way or a short, let wise men judge; and as he was traveling he heard a voice at the side of the road saying: 'Vasily the Luckless, where are you bound?' Vasily looked around him on all sides and said: 'Who is calling me?' 'I, the oak, am asking you where you are going.' 'I am going to King Dragon to collect rent for twelve years.' The oak said: 'If you arrive in time, remember to ask how much longer the oak must stand after standing for three hundred winters.'

"Vasily listened carefully and continued on his journey. He came to a river and sat in a ferryboat. The old ferryman asked him: 'Where are you bound, my friend?' Vasily told him what he had told the oak. And the ferryman requested him to ask King Dragon how much longer he would have to ferry, for he had been ferrying for thirty winters. 'I shall ask him,' said Vasily. He went on and reached the sea. A whale lay stretched out across the sea and people were walking and driving over her. When Vasily stepped on the whale, she said, 'Vasily the Luckless, where are you bound?' Vasily told her what he had told the ferryman and the oak, and the whale said, 'If you arrive in time, remember to ask how much longer I must lie here stretched across the sea, for people on foot and people on horseback have worn down my body to my ribs.'

"Vasily promised to ask and went on. He came to a green meadow; in the meadow stood a palace. Vasily entered the palace and went from room to room. Each was more splendid than the last. He went into the farthest room and found a lovely maiden sitting on the bed and weeping bitterly. When she saw Vasily, she rose up, kissed him, and said, 'Who are you and how did you happen to come to this accursèd place?' Vasily showed her the letter and told her that Marco the Rich had ordered him to collect twelve years' rent from King Dragon. The maiden threw the letter into the stove and said to

Vasily, 'Fool, you have been sent here not to collect rent but as drag-on's food. But tell me, what roads did you take? Did you see or hear anything on your way?' Vasily told her about the oak, the ferryman, and the whale. They had no sooner finished talking than the earth and the palace began to rumble. The maiden put Vasily into a chest under the bed and said to him, 'Now listen to my conversation with the dragon.' And saying this she went out to meet her lord.

"When King Dragon entered the room, he said: 'Why is there a Russian smell here?' The maiden said: 'How could a Russian smell get here? You have been flying over Russia and the smell is in your nostrils.' The dragon said: 'I am terribly exhausted. Pick the lice in my head.' And he lay down. The maiden said to him: 'King, what a dream I had while you were away! I was going along a road, and an oak cried to me: 'Ask the king how long I must stand here!' 'It will stand,' said King Dragon, 'until someone comes and kicks it with his foot; then it will be uprooted and will fall, and beneath it there is gold and silver—Marco the Rich does not have as much.'

"The maiden went on: 'And then I dreamed that I came to a river and the ferryman asked me how long he would have to ferry.' 'Let him put on the ferryboat the first man who comes to him, and push the boat away from the shore—and this man will ferry forever, and the ferryman can go home.' 'And then I dreamed that I walked across the sea on a whale, and she asked me how long she would have to lie there.' 'She shall lie there till she vomits up the twelve ships of Marco the Rich; then she will go down into the water and her flesh will grow again.' When King Dragon had said this, he fell sound asleep.

"The maiden let Vasily out of the chest and advised him thus: 'Do not tell the whale that she must vomit up the twelve ships of Marco the Rich until you have crossed to the other side. Likewise, when you come to the ferryman, do not tell him what you have heard until you have crossed the river. And when you come to the oak, kick it toward the east, and you will discover countless riches.' Vasily the Luckless thanked the maiden and went away.

"He came to the whale and she asked: 'Did he say anything about me?' 'He did. As soon as I cross I shall tell you.' When Vasily had crossed over, he said: 'Vomit up the twelve ships of Marco the Rich.' The whale vomited up the ships and they sailed forth, wholly unscathed; and Vasily the Luckless found himself in water up to his knees. Then he came to the ferryman, who asked: 'Did you speak about me to King Dragon?' 'I did,' said Vasily. 'First, ferry me over.' When he had crossed, he said to the ferryman: 'Whoever comes to you first, put him on the ferryboat and push it away from the shore; he will ferry forever, and you can go home.'

"Vasily the Luckless came to the oak, kicked it toward the east with his foot, and the oak fell. Beneath it he found gold and silver and precious stones without number. Vasily looked back and lo and behold, the twelve ships that had been thrown up by the whale were sailing straight to shore. And the ships were commanded by the same old man whom Vasily had met when he was carrying the letter of Marco the Rich to his wife. The old man said to Vasily: 'This, Vasily, is what the Lord has blessed you with.' Then he got off his ship and went his way.

"The sailors transported the gold and silver to the ships and then set out with Vasily the Luckless. Marco the Rich was told that his son-in-law was coming with twelve ships and that King Dragon had rewarded him with countless riches.

"Marco grew furious, hearing that what he desired had not yet come to pass. He had his carriage harnessed and set out to drive to King Dragon's palace and upbraid him. He came to the ferryman and sat in the ferryboat; the ferryman pushed it away from the shore, and Marco remained to ferry forever. But Vasily the Luckless came home to his wife and mother-in-law, began to live with them and gain increasing wealth, helped the poor, gave food and drink to beggars, and took possession of all the vast treasure of Marco the Rich."

hen the abbot finished telling his story he smiled and stood up, as if thinking of going to his bed now; but instead, with his head bowed, his right hand pushed inside his flowing left sleeve and his left hand pushed inside his flowing right sleeve, as he always stood except when he was praying, he walked over to the high, arched window that looked out at the stars above Suicide Leap; or perhaps it was the Leap itself he looked at, thinking about what the three of them had told him earlier. By the starlight one could see that his lips were trembling—it was quite pronounced—and one noticed that his head was slightly drawn in, like a turtle's or a chicken's, as if something had made him wince. He gave an abrupt headshake, as if in argument with himself; but precisely what the abbot might be thinking not even Chudu the Goat's

Son, who was half asleep anyway, with his pipe in his fist and his hat on his knees, could guess.

Prince Christopher the Sullen, still leaning on the mantel, toying with his brandy glass, said thoughtfully, glumly, "It's an interesting story. Yet one thing I don't understand, father."

"Yes?" said the abbot, turning from the window for a moment to scrutinize the prince. Armida, too, was watching Prince Christopher, for whatever she might think about poems and stories, she loved the sad shine she'd seen in the prince's eyes while he was listening.

"I don't understand why you've told it to us."

"Ah, that," said the abbot.

The fire in the hearth had died down to red coals, and there was no longer any sound of life outside the stone-walled room. The walls and beams had settled into blackness, so that the night sky beyond the high window was now brighter than where they sat. It was like looking out (Armida thought) from a funeral crypt, after everything has been decided; and the abbot's voice, for all its gentleness and kindness, was like some nagging, troublesome memory calling a ghost back, making things difficult again, confusing. She was inclined to rise to it, for the sake of the prince. For the sake of the prince she would happily reconsider everything. As for the dwarf, though he smelled like old laundry in an abandoned chickenhouse where there was garbage on the floor and the body of a cat, she would not be heartbroken if he should kill himself; but all the same it would be a loss to the world, there was no denying that; an incalculable loss, like the death of the last redwood. She tapped her lips with her fingertip, musing.

The abbot was saying: "I tell you the story—among other reasons—to remind you, dear friends, lanterns to my darkness, of a point that may possibly have slipped your minds—the moral, that is, that I called your attention to earlier: *Things are not always as they seem.*" He began pacing back and forth by the window, head bowed. "I know very little about the world, of course—" The abbot glanced shyly past his shoulder at them, gauging the effect his words were having, then started again: "I know, I say, very little about the world, cut off from things here on my mountain, so what I say may be foolishness. Nevertheless, it seems to me that there's a great truth in that tired old saw." He spoke the tired old saw one more time, lovingly, separating the phrases, and it came to Armida that he'd no doubt said it from the pulpit many times, if abbots did, as she was inclined to believe, sometimes preach: "*Things . . . are not always . . . as they seem.*"

Gazing up at the prince, his face just visible in the red coals' glow, Armida was surprised that she should see, even now, no trace of a smile. If he had any intelligence at all, it seemed to her, he'd see the humor in the abbot's old-womanish maunderings. Yet on the other hand it was touching to her that Prince Christopher should take in this hackneyed lecturing with such solemn innocence, such— what should she say?—sweet openness of soul. She was surprised— shocked—by the sudden recollection that the prince had spoken of suicide. "I mustn't let him," she thought. "That's all there is to it!"

She remembered all at once how the dwarf had bawled after her on the mountain road, "Armida, don't do it! Don't kill yourself!" and how he'd whooped and sobbed. She remembered his bellowing, "It *is* my business. It's very much my business!" She understood that now more clearly than she had at the time—and felt ashamed of herself. The tables had been turned on her: it was now Armida prepared to run shamelessly after the creature she loved, prepared to wail, as the dwarf had wailed, "Think of the people who love you! Think of how they'll feel!" Yet *could* she stop him from doing it? She was stronger than he, she had no doubt of that, and she was sure she could easily outsmart him. But her love for him put a constraint upon her: because she loved him, respected him as he couldn't respect himself, she was blocked, strange to say, from interfering. To control him, even for his own benefit, would be to diminish him, cheapen the value of his life—in his own eyes and even in hers. None of which was to deny that the prince's desire to kill himself was a sickness, as certainly a disease as those coughings and witherings and jerkings which the abbot each night knelt to cure. Nevertheless . . .

Armida wrung her hands, squinting into the glow of the coals beyond his legs. Because she loved him it was imperative that she be worthy of him, yes—be, insofar as was possible for her, the Dream Woman every man desires: soft and tender, gentle, shy as a violet in the woods. O cruel irony! Such a woman, of course, would have no possible means of preventing his self-destruction. He would brush her away like a feather, outwit her and storm off, wild-eyed, and be gone. Only if she could cause him to love her in return, spare his life for *her* sake . . .

Suddenly, looking up at his face, the features as still as the features of a lighted marble statue, Armida once again began to weep. No one noticed except Chudu the Goat's Son, and instantly he too began to cry. They both bent forward and shook with silent sobs, covering their faces with their hands, unaware that they were practically invisible in the room's thick darkness.

The abbot was droning on, just perceptibly smiling in the pale light the stars cast, occasionally gesturing with a mild little tilt of the head, the slight movement of a silhouetted arm. "That's the trouble, you see, with suicide. It may be that one has misapprehended the situation, that what seems so terrible and bitter in life as to make the race not worth the candle is in fact nothing more than some particularly seductive illusion, perhaps mere bad chemistry. A ripple of breath across the letter might in fact change all the writing. A little kick at the base of a tree might illuminate new golden options!"

The prince sighed profoundly. "Not in my case," he said.

The abbot, too, heaved a sigh, and once more, for an instant, a tremble seized his lips. "Yes yes, I can see it's desperate, in your case. And yet I wish—I hope not out of sinful curiosity—I wish I knew more of the particulars. It's many a grief for which God is relief and perhaps one or two for which *I* am."

"The tale can be quickly told," said the prince. "My father has sent me to hunt down the six-fingered man."

The old abbot's mouth dropped open in dismay. Startled out of his normal tranquillity, he seemed for an instant a completely different man. He waved his hand, as if quite involuntarily, in the direction of his eyes, and Armida, looking up past her own hands, that instant, noticed through her tears, or *thought* she noticed (but it was dark, as I've mentioned), that the long, pale, delicate fingers numbered six, not five! But she couldn't quite believe it, or failed to register—lost, as she was, in her own unhappiness and eagerly siding with the abbot's arguments, since he was trying to persuade Prince Christopher to continue living. Seeing (or imagining she saw) that sixth finger, Armida merely shivered, as if a bad dream had slipped into her mind and out again. And now the abbot's face was more gentle than ever, the tilt of his head more concerned.

"The six-fingered man!" he breathed. "God be with you, dear Prince!"

"I'm no fighter," said Prince Christopher. "I'd never have a chance, and my death would be vile and ignominious. I won't have it; I won't go to him. I'd far rather die by my own hand. I may not be free to live like a poet, but I can die like one!" He stood with his right hand pressed against his chest.

"Yes, I see," said the abbot. With sad eyes the abbot looked over in the direction of Armida and the dwarf (the dwarf was fast asleep), sitting in the darkness with their hands covering their faces. "Yes, you're right," said the abbot with a kind of groan, and began once more to pace. "You really do have no chance against the six-fingered man. How would you even find him? I understand he's very clever— murders people, or so rumor has it, and steals their identities. How's a man even to *locate* a fiend like that?" He shot a glance at the prince. "You have a clue?"

"Nothing," moaned the prince.

"Well, no matter anyway. You're right about this business, though it grieves me to say it. Heaven knows there's no percentage in your facing *that* man. —Of course he's not as young as he used to be, and there are always aspects of the situation that we're not aware of.

But you're right, yes. Safer to do battle with a thousand-year-old dragon."

The abbot stopped pacing as if he thought he'd heard a distant cry or something, and then his eyes lit up. He began to smile, excited, and came hurrying across the thick carpet toward the prince. He stopped a few feet short and looked up toward the corner of the ceiling, rapt, as if seeing a vision. "Now *there's* an idea!" he said.

Christopher the Sullen turned and looked doubtfully up in the direction in which the abbot was looking.

"Listen to me," the abbot said, moving closer and peering into Christopher's eyes. "No one could call it ignominious, now could they, if you lost your life in battle against a dragon? A man's not really *expected* to have a chance against a dragon. On the other hand, even while you're dying"—he rolled his eyes, made his voice more dramatic, waved the silhouette of an arm then quickly returned it to his cassock, "—even while you're gasping out your final breath, locked in mortal combat, you just conceivably might get in a lucky stab and leave the dragon so sorely wounded that—" His eyes flashed lightning and he gazed once more up at the corner of the room: "—so sorely wounded that he would eventually die. In a week or so, perhaps. Think of it! The lot of mankind would be significantly improved. You'd be famous throughout the world, throughout all history like Saint—" He pursed his lips; the name had slipped out of his memory. "Never mind, you get the drift."

"I," said Christopher the Sullen, and touched his collar-bone, "should fight a *dragon?*"

"Come come," said the abbot. "Use your imagination." He began pacing in a circle, into the hearth's glow, out of it again, into it, out of it. "You say you want to kill yourself. I disapprove, naturally, as a man of the cloth (though I might make exceptions for a terminal illness that involved great pain), but on the other hand I can readily see your point, now that you mention the notorious six-fingered man. Very well, if you feel you must kill yourself, why not do it nobly, as Lycurgus did, for the benefit of mankind? Moreover—pay attention now—you may be wrong about everything, as I've said to you before. For all you know, the six-fingered man may have died way last January, from stepping on an icy patch and falling on his head. Ha! You hadn't thought of that, had you, Prince Christopher! You'll never win your rightful place in history by choosing self-destruction rather than confrontation with a man who's in fact been dead for months. I don't say he *is*, mind you. Very well, though. Excellent. Now we're on the track."

The circle he was pacing became tighter.

"Dying in conflict with a dragon would be heroic, my boy! —And come to think of it, I know just the dragon for you, and not far off. You ever hear of Koog the Devil's Son?"

"Koog!" the prince whispered. The room went suddenly cold as ice. Armida gasped.

"You've heard of him I see," said the abbot. "Excellent! Excellent! *Now* we're on the track! He's old, this Koog, and crafty as the serpent he is. No question! On the other hand, his age is not all an advantage: he's hardly the dragon he once was, take my word! It's just barely possible—this is merely an opinion—that a man might take him, if he went at it right." He shot his face close to the face of the prince and whispered, looking back over his shoulder, "Old Koog's got a magic charm on him, you know."

"A charm," said Christopher the Sullen. His mouth was slightly open. He noticed this and closed it.

"Exactly. Nothing can harm him when he's in the dark of his cave. There was never a sword ever built that can scratch him. But out in the sunlight, ha!, that's quite another story! The question, of course, is how do you get a smart old dragon to come out in the sunlight where he's vulnerable?" The abbot stood nodding, fascinated himself by this conundrum.

Prince Christopher cleared his throat. He said, "Fighting dragons isn't basically my nature."

"Nonsense, my boy," said the abbot, almost nastily. Something crossed Armida's mind, too quickly for her to catch it. "This suicide was *your* idea, not mine," said the abbot. "I'm merely suggesting—"

"I'd been thinking of something rather quicker," said the prince, "and not too painful. Standing there in chainmail at the mouth of a cave, and taking the flame of a dragon head on—" He winced. He decided to pour himself more brandy, crossed quickly to the low, round table (the bottle and glasses faintly glinted in the starlight), and filled his brandy snifter.

The abbot came over to him. Armida could barely make out their two dark forms. Like a kindly old uncle the abbot put his arm around the prince, unless Armida was mistaken. "Come now, Prince," he urged, "let's think this through. I won't deny it could be painful. Of *course* it would be painful! Glory's not cheap!" Now both of them were pacing in a circle, into the hearth's dim light, out of it, in again

. . . Armida strained to see. "But let's not fool ourselves, my friend, about diving off a cliff. Believe me, I know about these things! First of all, there's the unspeakable terror involved. You may say it's more frightening to go charging against a dragon, but my friend, my dear friend, I doubt it. Think how it feels on the cliff-edge, standing looking down. True, we've all had the urge to fall. But how grim, how ghastly the actuality! How excruciatingly dreadful! And then there's the fall itself—first the unexpectedly painful banging of the heart. Many people, you know, die of heart attack long before they hit. And then the gasping for air. It's difficult to breathe, believe you me, hurtling down thousands of feet toward the rocks. And then the landing! Aie! How would you choose to hit? On your head—? Over in an instant, true, but can you actually conceive of— But landing on your feet would be no better, of course. Smash! In a split second your feet and legs are as nothing, fragile as glass, two blood explosions!, and the rocks are rushing toward your pelvis. Your back breaks—*wang!*— in a thousand places, your organs crash downward and upward and inward . . . Dear me! Bless me! Perhaps we should speak of drowning." The abbot stood stock-still, and the prince, too, stopped pacing.

"Drowning!" the abbot whispered. "The mind boggles! Are we seriously to believe that it's brief, painless? Behold the drowned fisherman's bugged-out eyes, his tightly clenched fists—though he floats, you may argue, like a babe in the womb! Time is subjective, as we've all observed. An instant can stretch out to a thousand years. And surely that's one vast *interminable* instant when the lungs wail for air and the water starts ringing and thundering in the drowning man's ears! Let us speak of poison."

When the prince interrupted, his voice was weak. "I realize it's difficult to kill yourself. You have to, you know, sort of trick yourself into it, one way or another, lie to yourself, become your own worst enemy, sneaking and shyly conniving against yourself, and even *then* it takes courage, a touch of craziness. Nevertheless, to walk up to a dragon, cool as you please—"

"Yes, good," said the abbot, "good, clear thinking. But let's *consider* that. We're assuming that to attack a dragon like Koog the Devil's Son is suicide. That may be our first mistake. It may very well be that you'll *kill* this Koog—that dwarf over there may know a trick or two, and our friend Armida may well have resources you haven't yet guessed. She told us herself that she's cunning and unnaturally strong. We must remember that. We must both of us *always* remember that, ha ha! So the dragon may prove a mere trifle after all. What do we really know, we poor finite mortals? You may find yourself slicing off the dragon's head—and dragging it back here for all of us to see—with such ludicrous ease that you're forced to guffaw—you and all your friends—at more ordinary mortals' trepidations. That's the thing, you see: the man who does battle with a dragon is, by definition, an exceptional man, necessarily a species of saint—indifferent about himself, a man concerned only about his brethren. Otherwise he wouldn't be there, you see. Precisely! He's a man 'born again' in a certain sense: a man who has learned that classic secret, that to save his life he has to throw it away. Now *there's* a new twist on suicide, my prince! You don't really throw away your life at all; instead you kill, as St. Paul says, the 'old' man—the carnal man, the self-regarding man—to give abundant life to the 'new.'

"Put it this way: why not try it? If you fight Koog the Devil's Son and win, against your wish—if you still even then, after that thrill, that glory, wish to end it all—come back to the monastery and I'll suggest some adversary more fierce yet, perhaps even— Monsters, sad to say, are never hard to come by. On the other hand, you owe it to yourself to take a crack at old Koog. That indifference to life that's gotten into you can be a powerful weapon for God's side. God loves the man who's indifferent about himself, the charitable man. That's the kind of fellow God looks after. Let me tell you a story."

Armida watched through spread fingers, more and more suspicious.

The Abbot's Second Tale

 certain king in a certain land had twelve daugh-
ters, each more beautiful than the last. Every
night these princesses went away, no one knew
where; and every night each of them wore out a
new pair of shoes. The king could not get shoes
for them fast enough, and he wanted to know
where they went every night and what they did. So he prepared a
feast, summoned kings and princes, noblemen, merchants, and the
humblest tradesmen, and, when they were assembled, said: 'Can
anyone solve this riddle of my daughters' shoes? He who solves it will
receive his favorite princess in marriage and half the kingdom as her
dowry.' However, no one had the nerve to undertake to find out
where the princesses went, except one needy nobleman, who said:
'Your Majesty, I will find out.' 'Very well, find out.'

"Soon the needy nobleman began to doubt and thought, 'What have I done? I have undertaken to solve this riddle, yet I do not know how. If I fail, the king will put me in prison.' Thus he walked along with a sad face. He met an old woman who asked him: 'Why are you so sad, my good man? Christ has died for us, and God is in his heaven.' He answered, 'Little mother, that's all very well, but how can I help but be sad as I walk? I have undertaken to find out for the king where his daughters go each night, and if I fail he will put me in prison.' 'Yes, that is a gloomy prospect,' said she, 'but not much more gloomy than continued poverty, and not much more gloomy than marriage to an obdurate princess. Make your peace with God, for earth is at bottom a silly place.' 'That is good advice; I will follow it.'

"The man went home in his threadbare cloak to his threadbare castle and called a priest and made his peace with God, and after that he felt more cheerful. The next day he met the old woman again, and she addressed him saying: 'I see you have made your peace with God.' 'Little mother,' he answered, 'so I have, and as the world rolls on, he has granted me his humor. I have a suspicion that the king will not be pleased to learn where his daughters have been going and wearing out their shoes, once he finds out; and though I may be miserable, so is the king, and surely an ordinary nobleman should smile and be cheerful when he has the luck of a king. It is true, however, that I'm no closer to solving the riddle than I was before.' 'Yes, that is a difficult task,' said the old woman. 'But it can be accomplished. Here is Saint Krasna's invisibility cap; with its help you can find out many things. Now listen well: when you go to bed, the princesses will give you a sleeping potion. Turn your face to the wall

and pour the drops into your bed, and do not drink them.' The nobleman thanked the old woman and returned to the palace.

"At nightfall he was assigned a room next to the bedroom of the twelve princesses. He lay on his bed and made ready to watch. Then one of the princesses brought him sleeping drops in wine and asked him to drink her health. He could not refuse, took the cup, pretended to drink, then turned to the wall and emptied the cup into his bed. On the stroke of midnight the princesses came to see whether he was asleep. The nobleman pretended to be sleeping so soundly that nothing could rouse him, but actually he was listening to every rustle. 'Well, little sisters,' said one of them, 'our guard has fallen asleep; it is time for us to go to the ball.' 'It is time,' said the others, 'high time!'

"They dressed in their best garments; the oldest sister pushed her bed to one side and disclosed a passage to the underground kingdom, realm of the accursèd king. They began to climb down the stairs. The nobleman quietly rose from his bed, donned his invisibility cap, and followed them. Accidentally he stepped on the youngest princess's dress. She was frightened and said to her sisters: 'Ah, little sisters, someone seems to have stepped on my dress; this is a bad omen.' But her sisters scoffed. 'Don't worry,' they said, 'nothing will happen to us.' They went down the stairs and came to a grove where golden flowers grew. The nobleman picked one flower and broke off a twig, and the whole grove rumbled. 'Ah, little sisters,' said the youngest princess, 'do you hear how the grove is rumbling? This bodes no good!' But again her sisters scoffed. 'Fear not,' they said, 'it is the music in the accursèd king's palace.'

"They came to a palace with a hundred rooms, each more evil

than the last, and were met by the king and his demonic courtiers. Infernal music began to play and they began to dance; they danced till their shoes were torn to shreds. The king ordered wine to be served to the guests. The nobleman took a goblet from the tray, drank the wine, and put the goblet in his pocket. At last the party was over; the princesses said farewell to their demon cavaliers, promised to come again the next night, returned home, undressed, and went to sleep.

"The next morning the king summoned the needy nobleman. 'Well,' he said, 'have you discovered what my daughters do every night?' 'I have.' 'Then where do they go?' 'To the underground kingdom, to the accursèd king, and there they dance all night.' The king went pale with rage and fear and summoned his daughters and began to question them: 'Where were you last night?' The princesses denied everything. 'We did not go anywhere,' they said. 'It must be that mice have destroyed our shoes.' The king said: 'Have you not been with the accursèd king? This nobleman testifies against you and is ready to offer proof.' 'Father, he cannot offer proof, for he slept all night long like the dead.' The needy nobleman drew the golden flower and the goblet from his pocket. 'Here is the proof.' The princesses had no choice but to confess everything to their father. He ordered the passage to the underground kingdom to be bricked up, and married his youngest daughter to the needy nobleman. From the beginning, the nobleman expected nothing of his wife, but as the years passed she gradually became all that his heart could have asked for."

o one spoke for a time when the abbot's tale ended. At last the abbot said, his voice slightly quaking, his gentle lips atremble, "There are three basic theories about the world, Prince. One is that it is essentially good, one is that it's essentially evil, and one is that it's neutral. What a wise man understands is that none of that is true. The world is a hodge-podge. Our human business, therefore—since our chief attribute is consciousness, and our greatest gift from God is, as Dante said, free will—our human business is to clarify, that is, sort things out, put the good with the good and the evil with the evil and the indifferent with the indifferent. Only when reality is properly sorted out can there be stability or hope for the future in either the individual or the state."

"Hmm," said the prince.

"That," said the abbot, "is the reason you have really no choice, as a prince and a feeling creature, but to kill the dragon Koog."

"I'm not sure I follow the logic," the prince said.

"What could be simpler, my dear prince? A dragon is a confusion at the heart of things, a law unto himself. He embraces good, evil, and indifference; in his own nature he makes them indivisible and absolute. He knows who he *is*. Surely you see that!"

For a moment the prince did not answer; no sound whatever came from him through the darkness. Then: "Perhaps I'm a little tired," he said.

"Put it this way," said the abbot. "Dragons all love life's finer things—music, art, treasure—the works of the spirit; yet in their personal habits they're foul and bestial—they burn down cathedrals, for instance, and eat maidens—and they see in their whimsical activities no faintest contradiction!" The words made the abbot gasp, as if the deep immorality of dragons was somehow personally threatening. Almost with a snarl the old man continued: "Dragons never grow, never change. Did you ever hear of a dragon committing suicide? Of course not! Believe me, nothing in this world is more despicable than a dragon. They're a walking—or flying—condemnation of all we stand for, all we pray for for our children, nay, for ourselves. We struggle to improve ourselves, we tortuously balance on the delicate line between our duties to society and our duties within—our duties to God and our own nature."

He grew more animated. The room was in absolute darkness now, the fire in the hearth had died completely, but Armida could hear the abbot pacing, hurrying back and forth, occasionally bump-

ing into the little table. He continued: "We human beings glimpse lofty ideals, catch ourselves betraying them, and sink to suicidal despair—despair from which only the love of our friends can save us, since friends see in us those nobler qualities we ourselves, out of long familiarity, have forgotten we possess. That, of course, is why the suicidal person is so difficult around his friends. I know all about these things, believe me. I don't live here at Suicide Leap for nothing! 'Get rid of all friends,' thinks the poor mad suicidal, 'and the end becomes a possibility.' So he insults his friends, teaches himself to hate them; yet even then secretly he hopes they will save him; even then he reaches out, bawls for new friends! Ah, these contradictions! Fiends are legion, we discover; our noblest hopes grow teeth and pursue us like tigers! Well, never mind; to be human is, inevitably, to hate oneself sometimes, to hunger for the perfect stability and in a way the perfect justice—or at least perfect punishment for our numerous imperfections—called death. What was I talking about? Ah! Yesss, the dragon. Old Koog."

He stopped pacing, stood perfectly still, lost in blackness. "A dragon, my dear prince, light of my life, has no such feelings as these I've just described. His existence is a malevolent joke on ours, a criticism, cosmically unfair. While the good man throws away his life to gain life, twists and strains and, with luck, transcends himself—by perilous battle achieves self-respect and the honest admiration of his neighbors and friends—and while the bad man with still a speck of decency throws away his for the love of that microscopic speck, the dragon flies out in the service of mad whim or sits at his ease for a thousand years on his useless emeralds and rubies, his gold cups and silver cups, and scornfully laughs! Does that really not disturb you, Prince Christopher? Do you feel no rage at all at a thing like that?"

After a moment Prince Christopher's voice came from the darkness: "Perhaps I should sleep on it."

"Yes, certainly," said the abbot. Quite suddenly, he showed his age: his voice was pure exhaustion. "Forgive me, I've kept all of you up too long." Without another word, he went to a door and threw it open. Feeble light crept in. "This way," said the abbot. The prince put down his brandy glass and came over to touch Armida's shoulder. She pretended to awaken, though in fact, of course, she'd been spying intently all the while. She sat up, flapped her lashes once or twice, then rose. The abbot stood waiting, hands in his cassock. Armida went to waken the dwarf. When her fingertips touched him, Chudu the Goat's Son gave a start and hurriedly turned himself into a book; then, fully awake, turned back into himself. "I dozed off," he said.

"It's time for bed," said Armida, and took a step toward the abbot. Now the dwarf, too, was on his feet, limping toward the light. The abbot led them down flagstoned hallways and across a stretch of grass to the monks' dormitory—there was a mumble of praying voices —and when they reached the place gave them three rooms. The dwarf said as Armida was about to close the door, "Did I miss anything?"

"I'm not sure," said Armida.

Something in her voice made Chudu the Goat's Son look harder at her face, but she was imitating her step-sister again, so there was nothing there to read.

"Good night," she said, and closed the door.

The dwarf moved on to his own room, the abbot standing in the dimness, watching with bright eyes. Yet his old face was drained, like a sick man's. Chudu called at the prince's door, "Good night, Prince." Christopher the Sullen was already sound asleep, still in all his clothes. "Good night," said Chudu to the abbot.

"Good night," said the abbot feebly, with a suggestion of a bow. Then the saintly abbot turned and, breathing heavily, just perceptibly dragging one foot, went his way.

he following morning Prince Christopher the Sullen announced that he'd decided to fight the dragon. He spoke of going alone, but Armida wouldn't hear of it, and since Armida insisted on going, the dwarf insisted that he, too, must go. The abbot ordered one of the monks to give Prince Christopher a map and said, "God bless you, my children." Another monk was sent to bring up Boy. The horse, when he saw the prince sharpening his sword and battle ax and putting an extra fine point on his lance, was extremely uneasy, but he said nothing. He considered not allowing the prince to mount, and he was downright cross when he discovered that today he was expected to carry Armida and the Goat's Son too; but it was a pretty day, with birds singing

everywhere, and except for a stamp of his right front hoof he made no protest.

Armida, leaning toward the prince's shoulder, said: "Did you bring your violin?"

"I always take my violin," said the prince, twisting around in the saddle to look at her. "Why?"

"No reason," said Armida, and smiled so stupidly that both Chudu and the prince felt vaguely suspicious. They kept their thoughts to themselves, however; the prince heaved a deep sigh, and poked the horse's side, very lightly, with his spurs.

Speedily a tale is spun; with much less speed a deed is done. When they had crossed the first mountain, and then a second and a third, they came to a wide green valley surrounded by forest, and at the end of the valley, set among wildflowers and bones, they beheld a cave. There was a stink far greater than Chudu's in the air, and though there were birds in every tree they were all of them as silent as fieldstones. The horse knew the cave of a dragon when he saw one, and he turned his head around and looked mournfully at the prince and wept a tear.

"Well, this looks like the place," said the prince, and bit his lips.

Armida and the dwarf dismounted, and the prince sat awhile more, biting his lips and sighing. Armida stood combing her long yellow hair, her pale wrist so limp it was a wonder she could manage to pull the comb. "Have you a plan?" she asked casually.

"Not really," said the prince. "I suppose when I get there something will come to me."

Armida glanced at him, pursed her lips, and went on combing. "How do you feel?" she asked.

"Oh–" the prince began thoughtfully. But he changed his mind and said no more.

Chudu the Goat's Son puffed at his pipe and batted his fists together nervously. He hadn't quite realized how much he liked Prince Christopher, and how sorry he would be when he was dead. He began to feel cross, and then downright angry, at the world in general. Against his carefully nurtured better nature he began to feel an impulse to destroy things—blast trees out of the ground, make the earth open up, or maybe stomp on his hat; but he controlled himself —as he always did, or almost always, when these dark urges came: he started counting. By the time he reached seven hundred thousand —he was counting very fast—he was mad as a hornet. If it were possible for a dwarf to kill a dragon he'd have done so on the spot; but dwarfs are impotent against dragons, no one knows why.

"Well," said the prince, and heaved another deep sigh, "I suppose I'd better get it over with."

"Good bye, Prince Christopher," said the dwarf, and he took his hat off and held it to his chest.

Armida burst out crying.

"Don't cry, Armida," said the prince gently. "It's not as bad as you think. I'll tell you something. It feels sort of good, to tell the truth. I would have said it was sentimental foolishness, but it feels really fine to be battling a dragon, with a beautiful maiden looking on. No fooling. It's the kind of thing a prince *ought* to do. Violin playing's all very well, and poetry, but I *am* a prince, after all, you know? I may not be very clever or very strong, but my *heart* at least is manly. I'm glad to have found that out."

"I'm proud of you, Prince Christopher," said Armida, trying hard to smile through her tears. "You *will* be careful?"

The prince laughed sadly. "How can a person be careful with a fire-breathing dragon?" He sighed one more time, gave them a wave, and started the horse toward the cave. A puff of smoke came out the entrance. Chudu batted his fists together, counting like lightning, and Armida made a kind of peeping sound, holding back sobs. When the horse had gone twenty paces, lifting his hooves high, like a parade horse, not from pride but because he was sick with fright and wanted to take the shortest steps possible, Armida called out, "I love you, Prince Christopher!" The prince turned and smiled and waved again and blew Armida a kiss. When the horse had gone forty paces, Armida suddenly threw down her comb and ran after him. "Wait!" she yelled. "*Wait!*"

The prince stopped and turned his horse sideways, letting her catch up. Chudu the Goat's Son took off after Armida, putting his pipe out as he ran by poking his finger in the bowl, and reached the horse two steps behind her.

"Prince Christopher, I have an idea," Armida said. Her bosom heaved, and in her embarrassment at having an idea she blushed scarlet.

"You do?" he said.

"Yes." She brushed her hair back. "Let *me* kill the dragon."

"You?" He looked baffled, then indignant.

"I know, I know, it's not what the beautiful maiden's supposed to do, and I'm ashamed of myself for suggesting it—you can see that for yourself. But *think* about it. No one will ever know except us three, and I'm *stronger* than you."

"You *are?*"

"Watch," she said. She glanced around for some suitable demonstration, then settled on the horse himself, took a deep breath, and picked up the horse in her arms with the prince still on it.

"Wow!" said the prince respectfully. The horse pawed the air and craned his head around to look.

She put him down again. "Also—I don't want to hurt your feelings, because I do love you, you know I do—but the truth is, I might be, well, smarter. I've thought of a plan."

The prince studied her, his expression so hurt they were afraid he might cry; then he turned away and picked at his beard, thinking. At last he said, "I can't do it. I mean it, Armida. If it ever got out that I sat back and allowed a beautiful maiden to—"

"But it *won't* get out! You know I'd die to protect your reputation. And *you* won't tell. What would that make *me* look like?"

"Yes, but there's the dwarf."

Armida laughed, though her eyes were still teary. Now she knew she had him. "The dwarf, you silly goose, loves *me*. He's even a little fond of you, I think."

The prince looked down sternly at Chudu. "Is that true?"

Chudu the Goat's Son bit his lip, then nodded.

The prince looked off for a long moment at the black entrance to the dragon's cave. "Well son of a gun," he said. After a while he said, "What's your plan?"

"We'll use teamwork," she said. "We'll gang up on him. Your

job is to play the violin. That will lure him out into the sunlight, where his magic charm won't help. And then the dwarf will go into a horrible tantrum and shape-shift and ruin things until the dragon charges him. And then I'll gallop in from the side on the horse and *mash, mash, mash, mash!*" With two hands she swung an imaginary sword. When she'd mashed four times, she held out the imaginary sword as a pointer. "Dead dragon."

The prince picked at his chin. His eyes lit up. "It just might work," he said, and almost smiled.

"Nothing doing!" said Chudu the Goat's Son fiercely. "It's not my nature to have tantrums."

"It's your *secret* nature, dwarf, and we all know it." She smiled as if she actually liked his secret nature, and she patted his hump. Perhaps in the back of her mind she was hoping it would bring luck.

"It's not fair!" yelled the dwarf, and snatched off his hat and began stomping it.

"That's good!" Armida said. "That's perfect! When the dragon comes, do that."

"Ouch, ouch, ouch!" yelled Chudu's hat.

And so, despite Chudu's protests, the thing was decided.

"I'll never live this down," the prince said, gloomily shaking his head; but he let them help him off with his armor, and Armida put it on. She swung the sword and ax a few times and hefted the lance to get the feel of it. Then they helped her up on the horse, and Christopher the Sullen got out his violin, tightened the bowstrings, and carefully tuned it. Armida rode the horse into the woods so the dragon wouldn't see him when he came barreling out.

"Now?" the prince called softly.

"Now!" Armida answered.

Christopher the Sullen began to play. Chudu's hair stood on end, it was so beautiful and tragic, and tears filled his eyes so he could barely see. He brushed them away with both hands to keep a bead on the cave-mouth. The music dipped and swooped like a mournful swallow, darting across the valley, gliding through the trees, and then, suddenly, there loomed the head of the dragon, peeking from the cave. The prince faltered, so horrible was the dragon's look, then went on playing. The head snaked out farther, rising up into the sky and weaving as it came; it was wide and flat, like a poisonous snake's, and the glittering tusks in its partly opened mouth were nine feet long. The eyes were black mirrors that reflected the whole valley, and the scales on the neck and chest and belly, like the bristles on his pate, were of colored metal plate and all brighter than lightning. Back and forth the head moved, slowly, terribly, like the head of a cobra; and now one foot came out into the valley—talons like a monstrous eagle's—and after it a second foot. For a moment it seemed that the music alone would bring Koog into the sunlight, but with his two feet exposed he paused, for profound caution was in Koog's nature, and his terrible head stopped moving. He seemed to meditate.

At a hundred and forty-four thousand, Chudu stopped counting and went into his rage.

"*YARG! WOOF! YOWL!!*" bellowed Chudu the Goat's Son, and the noise was like a hundred volcanoes. The dragon jerked his head back. Chudu ran forward, trembling in his fury like a thrashing machine. Never in his life had he felt such pure, glorious anger. He turned himself into a thunderball and set a tree on fire, then turned

himself into a mad bull elephant and stomped the ground until it split in a great wide seam and he almost fell in. He turned himself into a sheep and ran straight at the cave-mouth, then turned into a hawk and sped away just in time as the dragon spit flame and the sky rained soot. He turned himself into a laughing hyena and laughed at the dragon with bitter scorn, then turned himself into a silly old woman in a rowboat, drinking gin. He turned himself into a cat, then a bat, then a mouse, then a house, then a huge, four manual pipe-organ.

The dragon couldn't stand it. He plunged into the valley with a terrible roar and a great belch of fire and came bounding toward Chudu with his vast, webbed wings half-extended. Chudu turned into thin air and was gone from sight.

Out came Armida and the horse full tilt, the lance running straight as an arrow, cradled in her arm. The dragon turned sharply and raised his head to spit fire, but too late, his enemy was upon him, and before he could even cry out at her in righteous indignation *I AM KOOG!*, the lance went straight through him, and Armida had jumped up and was standing on the saddle, swinging with the broadsword, cutting off his head. It fell like some colossal boulder—the horse leaped back—and the mirroring eyes went unfocused. Chudu turned back into himself and lay panting in the grass.

"We did it!" cried Armida, and waved her triumphant sword. She galloped back over to the prince and kissed him, and then, from pure high spirits, kissed the dwarf.

After they were rested, Armida gave the prince his armor again and they tied a rope around the dragon's head so they could drag it behind the horse. Then they started back.

As they were approaching the Ancient Monastery, the prince said soberly, "There's something I think I should tell you two."

"Yes?" Armida said and leaned sideways and forward so she could look past his shoulder at his face.

"I've changed my mind. I think I won't kill myself after all. The abbot was right."

"That's wonderful!" cried Armida. "Oh, Prince Christopher, that's *wonderful!*"

"And I don't want you to kill yourself either, all right?"

"Anything you say," said Armida, and put on her silly look. "You know I wouldn't dare disobey you."

Chudu was so happy he forgot that he too had intended to kill himself.

When they were almost at the gate of the monastery, Armida said, "There's something I ought to tell you two, too."

The prince twisted around to look at her.

"I think the abbot," said Armida, "has six fingers on each hand."

The horse began to tremble.

"But don't be frightened," she added quickly, and gave them a wink. "I have a plan."

hey found the abbot reading and thoughtfully pondering a book about a murderer. The abbot, as it happened, had hundreds of such books. He quickly put it down and stuck his hands into his cassock and asked the travelers their news.

"So you've killed the dragon," said the abbot when they'd told him. "Incredible!" He looked at Prince Christopher with new respect, then called one of his monks to him. "Brother Will," he said, his old eyes bright and his gentle lips trembling, "gather the brothers together and get all the monastery wagons, and go to the cave where old Koog used to be, and gather up all his treasures and bring them to the monastery."

"So that's why you wanted the dragon dead," said Christopher the Sullen.

"Naturally, my son," said the abbot, smiling. "But it's not for ourselves, it's for the poor and needy. Of course it all rightfully belongs to you, I'm well aware of that, and however much or little you may want of it—"

"No no," said the prince with a wave. "I have everything I need back at the palace. Greed's the root of all evil."

"You're a wise young man," said the abbot. Then he said, "Come, let's get you out of that armor and into something softer."

After they had all changed, he took them to the stone-walled chamber with the fireplace—for suppertime was past—and nodded toward the wine and warmed-up food the holy brothers had laid out for them. The three ate and drank to their hearts' content, and the abbot looked on approvingly. Armida used her knife and fork and spoon with such delicate grace no one would have believed, who had not seen it, that such a frail wisp of a girl could have slain a dragon. It seemed unlikely that she could lift an iron dagger, let alone a knight's long lance. When the abbot tried politely to engage her in conversation, her answers and comments were so shy and foolish that even Prince Christopher the Sullen was forced to smile.

After they'd finished eating, the abbot nodded in the direction of the brandy and invited them to help themselves. "Would you pour it for me?" asked Armida in a whispery, girlish voice, and smiled prettily. "I never know how much is proper."

The abbot, who preferred to keep his hands where they were, buried in the folds of his cassock, smiled at her and said, "I'm unworthy of such an honor! Let the prince pour. That would be more fitting."

"I'll be glad to pour," said Prince Christopher, and gave Armida a solemn wink.

When they all had their brandy, except of course the abbot, the abbot said, with such warmth and good-heartedness that even the dwarf was momentarily persuaded that Armida must surely be mistaken about the monk's six fingers, "Tell me how you accomplished this great feat, my dear prince, root of all my happiness! How I wish I'd been there to see it! Is it possible—" He smiled and leaned confidentially toward the prince. "Is it possible you had help from the dwarf? I suggested myself, if I remember correctly, that the dwarf might conceivably know a trick or two. A little shape-shifting, perhaps? A little bumble and confusion?"

Prince Christopher chuckled, though his look was still mournful. "Oh, he's not *that* kind of dwarf. He may have done such things on rare occasions in his youth, but magic is against his principles. He's the soul of gentleness and reason, as you'd know if you traveled with him. He refuses even to play chess—game of too much aggression."

"How odd," said the abbot, and critically studied the dwarf. "Yet surely he told us in this very room that his reason for considering suicide was his potential destructiveness!"

"That's always been his one great fear, yes," the prince said, gazing sadly and kindly at the dwarf. "That's why it's so important to him never to let go. I admire him for it, though I confess, when I was fighting the dragon there were moments when I would have been grateful for a little noisy magic. But no matter! Here we are, safe and sound."

"So you are," said the abbot with satisfaction. "And has my little cure worked?"

"Cure?" said the prince.

"Surely you've realized by now why it was that I proposed that mission. I predicted, didn't I, that you might come out of it un-scathed, thanks to your indifference to your personal welfare and your princely concern about others?"

"I believe you did predict that."

"Exactly! My thought, you see, was that if you succeeded with the dragon you might shake off that notion of suicide."

The prince glanced at Armida. "So *that* was your game."

"I can't deny it," said the abbot. "And I hope you'll tell me I was successful."

Prince Christopher laughed with him, a trifle morosely, and stud-ied the abbot's face. "Surely Armida must be wrong this once," he thought. "Yes," he told the abbot, "you were successful; we've aban-doned the idea."

"Bless you!" said the abbot. "Perhaps you'd reward me for my favor, then, with a little violin music."

The prince sneaked a glance at Armida; she just perceptibly nodded. "If you insist," said the prince with a troubled frown. "I no longer think of myself, to be truthful, as a violinist. I'm a swordsman, basically, as the six-fingered man will soon learn to his grief. But since you ask, I'll go get my fiddle." He went off at once and before long returned with the instrument. Deftly he screwed the bow tight and tuned the violin-strings, then looked off into space for a moment, deciding what to play. At last he put the instru-ment to his chin and, with a long sweet note on the D-string, began.

"Beautiful," murmured the abbot when Christopher the Sullen had played a phrase or two, and he closed his eyes, wagging his head with the music, and listened with all his heart.

Christopher the Sullen played for hours that night, and the fol-

lowing day he played again for the abbot, a long time or a short time, all the while insisting that he was really a swordsman, and sometimes, between rhapsodies, he would make what seemed an absentminded little thrust or parry with the bow. Though he was the worst of swordsmen in actual combat—mainly because he had no courage and no interest—he'd had excellent training and looked thoroughly professional, so that the abbot, watching, could not be at all certain that the prince wasn't dangerous. The dwarf all the while sat placidly smiling, stroking his long beard, sometimes bumping his watch on the chair-arm, as if trying to get the thing going and refusing to use magic. Armida smiled and simpered and batted her eyelashes and once, pretending to have seen a mouse, screamed and panicked.

These ruses worked so well that, despite all they'd told him, by the third day the abbot paid attention to no one but Prince Christopher—gently, mystically smiling at the prince, but watching like a hawk. On that day the brethren returned with their wagonloads of treasure. There were more precious jewels, more gold coins and silver coins, more beautiful works of art than even Chudu the Goat's Son had ever before seen, though it is part of the business of a dwarf to keep track of old treasures. The monks parked the wagonloads of treasure in the barn, held mass, then began to prepare supper.

Meanwhile, the saintly old abbot prayed for the crippled and sick until all of them were cured. Armida, the prince, and the dwarf observed. "Notice," Armida whispered, "how he holds his hands to pray."

The prince bent forward and did as he was told. As the abbot prayed, only four fingers and a thumb on each hand peeked out from the darkness of the cassock's sleeves; but the prince was almost certain that one more finger on each hand was tucked under, out of sight. Nevertheless, whether or not he was the six-fingered man, the abbot was curing the sufferers. If he was truly that master of disguise, that notorious murderer, how could this be? Armida herself was inclined to doubt, for the hundredth time, that she was right. She cursed, too softly for the others to hear, and bit her knuckles and waited for a sign. If her plan was successful, it would come.

That night, as usual, the abbot retired with the three friends to the stone-walled chamber for brandy, talk, and music. The prince played his fiddle for an hour and more; then he said—for it was part of the plan that the prince do most of the talking, saying exactly what Armida had coached him on, so that he might seem to the abbot to be dangerously clever—"Father, we've immensely enjoyed your hospitality; but I'm afraid we must leave tomorrow. I must hunt down the six-fingered man."

The abbot smiled with his usual gentleness. "I hardly know whether to wish you luck or not," he said. "Surely if you find him he'll kill you on sight. But then, how can you find him—unless *he*, God forbid, should find *you?*"

"That's an interesting thought," said the prince, "and I admit I've thought it. It's his way, I'm told, to study a man for a few days, then steal his identity. It's entirely possible that from some nook or cranny he may be watching me even now, preparing to slaughter me like a goose. But I'm no child. I must take my chances."

"You're a brave young man, my dear prince, glory of my life," said the abbot. "I admire you for it. Perhaps you'll get together after all, this fiend and you, and perhaps you'll actually kill him somehow, though I doubt it. The six-fingered man will be thankful that finally it's over, if he has any sense."

"I doubt that he's feeling that much misery," laughed the prince.

"Perhaps not," said the abbot. "If he does, it's nobody's fault but his own. That man should have ended it all long since. The older he gets the more surely he must see that he's detestable."

"I really do doubt that he thinks that way," the prince said.

"Perhaps not, perhaps not," the abbot agreed, nodding. "Yet he's a master imitator, we're given to understand. Surely he's imitated good men, from time to time, and accidentally picked up at least a touch of decent conscience. Imitate anything long enough—gaze at anything long enough with a careful eye—and you have a tendency to become it, or at very least a tendency to respect it. I might take the case of painting. There was a time, you'll remember, when people hated Nature. When they found Nature unavoidable, in a particular painting, they transmuted all that garish green to brown. Forced to live in the country, they transformed lawless Nature into formal gardens. Then an outlaw generation of young painters came along and painted mountains 'as they are'; and a gasping generation of young poets came along and wrote sweet love-songs to Mont Blanc. Rich merchants with big houses in the centers of their villages learned the subtle art of turning half an acre to a forest—'natural' pools, concrete reindeer. What had happened? Exactly! Painters had begun imitating the world as they saw it, a world of—incredible!—fat ladies with their clothes off, green mountains, majestic bears—and the world began to imitate the paintings. Make no mistake, make no mistake! The mimic is doomed to become what he mimics, or doomed unless a miracle of good fortune intervenes. It's like the story of the miser."

"Miser?" said the prince.

Armida sighed.

The Abbot's Last Tale

There was once a wealthy merchant named Nikita the Mean. One day as the world rolled on he went out for a walk and on his way saw an old beggar who was asking for alms. 'For Christ's sweet sake, good merchant, give me at least a little pittance!' cried the beggar. Nikita the Mean tipped his nose up and passed him by.

"But a poor peasant who followed behind him felt pity for the beggar and gave him a kopek. Rich Nikita saw that everyone was watching and felt horribly ashamed; so he stopped and said to the peasant, 'Listen, little brother, lend me a kopek. I want to give something to the beggar but I have no small change.' The peasant gave Nikita a kopek and asked: 'When shall I come to collect my loan?' 'Come tomorrow.'

"The next day the poor man went to the rich man for his kopek; he entered the broad courtyard. 'Is Nikita the Mean at home?' 'He is,' said Nikita's wife. 'What do you want of him?' 'I have come for my kopek.' Nikita the Mean heard this and went and hid under the bed and told his wife to tell the peasant that now that she looked she found he wasn't home after all, the peasant should come tomorrow. 'Come tomorrow,' said Nikita's wife; 'now that I look I find he's gone.' So the following day the peasant came again, and this time he came upon Nikita himself, standing by the gate, for there was no time for Nikita to run away. 'I have come for my kopek,' said the peasant. 'Ah, little brother,' said Nikita, 'come and see me some other time. I have no small change just now.' The poor man bowed low and said: 'I will come next week.' The following week he came a third time and was told: 'Forgive me, dear brother, but again I have no small change. If you have change for a hundred rubles, I can give you a kopek. If not, come next month.' A month later, the poor man went again to the rich man. When Nikita the Mean saw him through the window, he said to his wife: 'Listen, wife, I will undress completely and lie under the ikons; and you cover me with a shroud and sit down and lament me as though I were dead. When the peasant comes for his loan, tell him that I died today.'

"The wife did as her husband commanded; she sat down and shed burning tears. The peasant came into the room and she asked, 'What is it, dear brother?' 'I have come to collect my loan from Nikita the Mean,' answered the peasant. 'Ah, little peasant, Nikita the Mean wished you a long, happy life! He has just died.' 'May angels carry him to heaven!' said the peasant. 'And since he was a good man and gave money to beggars, let me do something for him. Permit me to

wash his body.' Before the wife could object, the peasant snatched a kettle of boiling water and poured it over Nikita the Mean. Nikita could hardly stand it; he gritted his teeth and jerked his feet. The peasant pretended not to notice and washed the body and prepared it for burial. To the wife he said, 'Buy a coffin and bring it here, and we will put the body in it. And if I know anything at all about my friend Nikita he would not want to be buried without his money, so we will also put all Nikita's money in the coffin, packed around his body, and then we will bear it to the church.' The wife had no choice but to go and get a coffin, and the peasant did as he had said he would. He crammed in Nikita's gold and jewels and his ivory boxes and silver clasps, and he placed Nikita's golden saber over the body, and closed the lid. They carried the coffin to the church and the peasant began to groan and read the psalter over him. And Nikita's wife stood beside him and wept burning tears.

"Dark night came. Suddenly a window opened and thieves broke in, bringing with them all that evening's loot, silver coins and gold coins, silver and gold candlesticks, and cups of solid amber, treasure enough to keep a king. The thieves ran straight to the casket to use it for a counting table. The peasant and Nikita's wife ducked down quickly behind the altar while the thieves counted their treasure and put it all in sacks. Then the thieves opened the casket and discovered, to their surprise, the wealth of Nikita the Mean, all packed around the body. 'This is a lucky night for us,' they cried. 'Praise God!' And they sent out for more bags and began putting into them all Nikita's treasure. Nikita gritted his teeth in agony, but he would not cry out because there was always the chance that the thieves might be taken and the treasure recovered, whereas that kopek would be gone for-ever if that peasant got ahold of it. Soon the treasure was all bagged and tied except for Nikita's golden saber, and this the thieves began to quarrel about. The peasant suddenly jumped out and cried, 'Let me settle this dispute! Whoever cuts off the dead man's head shall have the saber!'

"At this Nikita the Mean jumped up, beside himself with fear, and just in the nick of time, too! If he'd played dead another half second he would have been deader than he wanted. The thieves, too, were frightened, and abandoning the money, both Nikita's and their own, they took to their heels. 'Now, little peasant,' said Nikita, 'let us share the robbers' money, and since I worked the harder for it, I shall have the most.' They shared it as Nikita the Mean thought right, and even so, both of them got a great deal. 'And how about my kopek?' said the poor man. 'Ah, dear brother,' said Nikita, 'you can see for yourself I have no small change.' And Nikita the Mean never did return the kopek, but lived happily ever after."

t's an interesting story," said the prince, after a nod from Armida, "but I'm not sure why you tell it."

"Well, not solely for the moral," said the abbot with a smile. "As the world rolls on, I grow less and less interested in the moral. But it's true, as the story teaches us, there's a curious rigidity in human nature, especially when we get older. It's easier to heal the sick or give blind men sight than it is to part a miser from his kopek—or a murderer from his knife. The miser may hate himself, as did Nikita the Mean; the murderer, if he has any sensitivity at all, may become, in his own eyes, so thoroughly repugnant that he spends half his days and nights out at the edges of cliffs, praying to God for the nerve to jump. Nevertheless, you know, a habit's hard to break. You get a vision, one way or another, of what you'd like to be—perhaps a vision of yourself as the world's greatest monster, if you happen to encounter the right books and friends. If you decide, for one reason or another, you don't like that, you discover to your sorrow, if you've worked very long at becoming what you are, the new vision's impotent to change you."

Prince Christopher sipped his brandy, his eyebrows raised. "And this may have happened, you think, to the six-fingered man—that is, he's become, to himself, repugnant?"

"I could swear to it, my prince, happiness of my days! Not that that makes him less dangerous, of course. On the contrary, despair gives a murderer an advantage. We spoke earlier, you recall, of the advantage indifference to life might give you with the dragon. But a murderer who's broken all God's laws and man's and has no hope for his soul—who *has*, in fact, no soul—that murderer has the same advantage you had. *Had*, I must add, and have no longer. You've gotten interested again; you've abandoned your idea of committing suicide. That makes you vulnerable. He, on the other hand, the six-fingered man, of what concern is it to him which one of you dies, whether you die or he dies? His hand, therefore, will not tremble. His eye will not misjudge."

He glanced at Armida, who sat watching in what seemed worried silence, with her eyes now on Prince Christopher, now on the abbot.

"Nor is that all," said the abbot. "The six-fingered man is more solitary even than Koog the Devil's Son. Oh, he has his men. Cutthroats, purse-snatchers. He could see them all hanged in a minute and never blink an eye. He has no kind, stern father, concerned, as yours is, that his son be worthy of the world's respect and friendship. No mother, such as yours, who fusses over him, praising his weaknesses, begging him to put on galoshes when it rains, swooning with pride and pleasure when he plays the violin or composes a lyric. The six-fingered man has nobody; nothing snarls his feet. In the blackness of his despair he has cut away all ties. You, on the other hand, have not only your parents and Armida and the dwarf, you have a whole wide kingdom of admirers who love you as I do. You have more friends than most men to worry about. So you'll glance around behind you, when you meet with the man, making sure that Armida's out of reach and the dwarf not sleeping. Your hand will tremble, my son; your eye will misjudge."

"Perhaps that's so," said the prince. "We'll have to see."

Armida said, "He'll just have to do his best, father."

"Yes he will," the abbot said and smiled. "He certainly will." Now he turned away and walked to the window to look out, whether at the stars and the full moon or down at the cliff I cannot say. "It's a beautiful night," he remarked. "Would anyone care to walk out in it?"

"That would be lovely!" Armida said. She sat forward in her chair, ready to get up.

"Let's do it then," the abbot said. "We could walk out by Suicide Leap, if you're interested, and you can gaze down at the boulders and be thankful you're not jumping." He laughed oddly, then moved across the room toward the door. Armida and the dwarf rose behind him to follow, and the prince came last. Soon they were at the rear of the monastery, at the edge of the cliff. The stars were like thousands of bits of ice in the sky; the wind at their backs was cold. "I should have brought a wrap," thought Armida, for her long white dress was thin. She walked with the dwarf close to the edge and peeked over— the dwarf reached up and caught hold of her hand—then backed away again, dizzy. The prince stayed where he was, several paces from the edge.

Safe in the darkness of a cypress hedge, the abbot took Prince Christopher's arm. "I want you to know, my prince, light of my life, I've enjoyed these few hours we've had together. I don't know when I've enjoyed anything more. I like a conversationalist who makes me think, but that is the least of it. I'll say no more. And you, my two friends—" he nodded to Armida and the dwarf—"you're wonderful company, both of you. I've never known better. I wish this time we're having could last for all eternity. For various reasons, however—sad, sad reasons!—I must say—" He broke off, dropped Prince Christopher's arm, and moved away a little. Almost imperceptibly, Armida drew more erect, and Chudu the Goat's Son—his lips moving, for he was counting like lightning—tipped his head forward, ready to charge like a bull. (None of this, unfortunately for him, did the abbot see. Fool that he was, he was carefully not looking, watching no one at all but Prince Christopher.)

When he had walked five or six paces from the prince, up the hill from him, toward the dark, looming monastery, the abbot turned around. In the moonlight his smile seemed no longer kind and gentle but transformed to a ghastly grimace. He had his hands at his sides, unhidden now. "There *is* one thing more I can do for you, Prince," the abbot said. "You're looking for the notorious six-fingered man." He paused dramatically (he'd spent years on the stage), then stretched his hands out so the three of them could see. "Here he stands!" he said. He held his hands out a moment longer, making sure the shock registered. Then, as if casually, he moved his right hand to the front of his cassock, reached down inside the collar and, with a lightning-quick motion, drew out a sword. Armida gasped in spite of herself and clasped her hands together at the waist. With her left hand she reached two fingers down into her belt for the penknife she'd hidden there.

"You can't do this!" cried Prince Christopher, stepping back from the abbot's sword. "I'm defenseless!"

"How thoughtless of you," said the six-fingered man, and laughed. He began moving toward the prince, backing him toward the cliff. Still Armida and the dwarf hung fire.

"Tell me just one thing," said the prince. "What happened to the real abbot? And also, how does it happen that you can cure the sick?"

The six-fingered man continued slowly toward him, smiling eerily and moving the sword from side to side with a swing of the wrist. "The saintly abbot and all his holy monks are dead. All dead. They await you at the bottom of the cliff. Our band has replaced them. As for the miracles, the old man never knew himself how he did them, so how should I? I simply mimic: I do exactly what he did, to the last microscopic tremor." He made as if to lunge, and the prince glanced behind himself and made a whimpering noise. Up the hill, above them, the evil monks were gathering at the corners of the monastery, and every one of them had a sword or a mace, glinting in the moonlight. When they were all assembled they began to come down toward the cliff-edge, walking slowly, more silently than owls.

"Tell me this," said the prince. "*Why* do you heal the sick? It seems a queer thing for a murderer to do."

It seemed to Armida that the false abbot blanched. His mouth gave a jerk—a fierce nervous tic. "Don't ask me that," he said.

"But I *do* ask it," said the prince, and stopped backing up. He'd reached the edge.

The six-fingered man said, swinging the sword from side to side more quickly now, switching it, in fact, "I don't *know* why I heal the sick. It's just one of the things the old abbot used to do, so it's necessary, a part of my act. And I like it."

"You *like* it?" Chudu the Goat's Son broke in. "You?—a homicidal maniac?"

The six-fingered man glanced at him, then back at the prince. Armida now began to move, very slowly, her white dress rippling in the mountain wind. Little by little she was working her way around behind the man. The six-fingered man said: "It makes me *feel* good. I don't pretend to understand it. I feel light, as if in a minute I might levitate, and sometimes I hear music—a women's choir. I feel myself getting warm, practically burning up; but it's pleasant, downright glorious. Sometimes I smell incense. Don't ask me any more, I don't want to think about it. When it's over and I'm my normal self again, it's terrible—terrible! All I can think about is jumping off the cliff."

And now, as if at some signal from Armida, Chudu the Goat's

Son rushed straight at the murderer, bellowing with gleeful, bound-less rage, and the exact same instant Armida screamed "*Yi!*" like a wild insane savage and leaped six feet onto the murderer's back. The Goat's Son turned into a huge anaconda and wrapped his fat body around the murderer's two arms, and squeezed and constricted till the six-fingered man dropped the sword. Armida, by this time, had her knife at the man's throat, and the prince, by this time, had picked up the sword and was stabbing him with it. (He had no choice; no jail in the world could hold the six-fingered man.)

"Tricked!" cried the six-fingered man, and burst out crying. "The dwarf *did* do magic, and it was the *girl* that killed the dragon! I knew it all the time!"

To hush him before anyone could hear what he was saying, Christopher the Sullen cut his head off and—with the same swipe, by accident—cut off one six-fingered hand. He put the hand in his pocket. The head, as soon as it hit the ground, cried: "Praise God!"

For an instant, the Suicide Mountains fell silent, as if holding their breath, amazed.

Now the monks all came running, shouting and swearing oaths. "*Let them all be mules!*" shouted Chudu the Goat's Son, and at once they were all mules, and their weapons fell clattering. They stopped running and turned and stared at each other and a few began to kick.

"Good thinking," cried Armida. "We'll hitch them up to the treasure wagons and drive them to the palace, and when we get there we can change them back to people and chuck them in the dungeon!" The prince, Armida, and the dwarf began rounding up the mules.

Even with Chudu's magic they were hard to catch, but by the time the first cock crowed and the sky began to light, the last of them was captured and hitched securely to his treasure wagon.

"There's one last thing we must do before we leave," said the prince. "We must bury the six-fingered man."

"That's true," Armida said. "For all his evil, he had good in him, too, and he relieved the suffering of as many people as he murdered. It would be wrong to leave his bones for the crows to pick."

So they left the mules to stand waiting in the barn, chewing oats and hay, and walked around to get the body and carry it to a burial place. Lo and behold, when they reached the green slope where the body had lain there was no sign of it, neither clothes nor blood; but there was a new-born babe sitting picking the grass and trying to eat it, getting dirt in its mouth but not minding in the least, burbling and larbling and chirping like a sparrow. When they picked it up it laughed at them happily, and they noticed it had only one hand, and the hand had six fingers.

Much puzzled, they carried the babe along with them and set him down under a tree while Armida and the dwarf got out the wagons and Prince Christopher the Sullen went to the horsebarn and saddled his horse. When Boy was saddled the prince got up in the saddle with the babe, and Armida and the dwarf climbed up into the seat of the lead wagon, with the rest of the mules and wagons tied one after another behind, each wagon richer than the last, and they started for the palace.

"Does it talk yet?" Armida called forward to the prince.

"I don't know." He asked the baby: "Can you talk yet?"

The baby smiled merrily and nodded and began to talk:

The Baby's Tale

In a certain village there lived two brothers, a rich one and a poor one. The rich one lived square in the center of town and had a huge wooden house and was a member in good standing of the merchants' guild. But the poor one, more times than I care to tell, had not even so much as dry bread to eat, and when his little children wept and begged for food he had nothing at all he could give them, but bade them suck on rags. From long before sun-up to long after dark, the poor man struggled like a fish against ice, but he could never earn anything.

"One day he said to his wife, 'I will go to the center of town and ask my brother for help.' 'Go then,' said his wife, 'but your brother is a pig and will not help you.' He came to the rich man and said, 'Ah, my own brother, help me a little in my misery. My wife and children are without food, they go hungry for days on end.' His brother answered him, 'Work in my house for a week, then perhaps I will help you.' What could the poor man do? He set to work, swept the yard, curried the horses, carried water, and chopped wood. At the end of the week the rich brother gave him one loaf of black bread. 'This is for your work,' he said. 'Thank you even for that,' said the poor brother. He bowed low, till his head was against the floor, and was about to go home. 'Wait,' said the rich man. 'Come and visit me tomorrow and bring your wife with you. Tomorrow is my birthday.' The poor man was ashamed and said, 'Brother, I don't belong there, you know it well. Your other guests will be merchants in glittering boots and fur coats, and I wear plain linden bark shoes and a wretched gray caftan.' 'Never mind, just come. There will be a place for you.' 'Very well then, brother, I will come.'

"The poor man returned home, gave the bread to his wife, and said, 'Listen, wife, we are invited to a feast tomorrow.' 'A feast?' she said, 'who has invited us?' 'My brother,' came the answer. 'Tomorrow is his birthday.' Though the wife was normally a patient woman, she spit out the window. 'Your brother is a spider and a weasel and an eel, but very well, we will go.'

"Next morning they rose and went to the center of town. They came to the rich brother's house, wished him a happy birthday, and sat down on a bench. Many prominent guests were already at the table, the mayor and all the aldermen, merchants and wealthy tradesmen, and a distant relative of the king. The host served them all abundantly, but he forgot even to think about his poor brother and sister-in-law, and did not offer them anything; they just watched the others eating and drinking, and were too ashamed to beg to be given food. The dinner was over, the guests began to rise from the table and to thank the host and hostess. The poor man too rose from his bench and bowed to his brother, so low that his head was against the floor. The guests went home drunken and merry, noisily singing songs.

"The poor man, however, walked with a painfully empty stomach. He said to his wife, 'Let us sing a song too, wife.' She said: 'Eh, you blockhead! The others are singing because they ate savory dishes and drank mead and wine to their hearts' content. What gives you the idea of singing?' 'Well,' he said, 'after all I have been at my brother's feast. I am ashamed to walk without singing. If I sing, everyone will think that I too had a good time.' 'Well, sing if you must, old fool,' said his wife, 'but I won't.' The peasant began singing a song and he heard two voices. He stopped and turned to his wife. 'Was it you who accompanied me in a thin voice?' 'What is the matter with you?' she said. 'I wouldn't sing a note. I didn't have a good time at all and your brother is a carp.' 'Then who was it?' he asked. 'I don't know,' said she, 'but sing again and I will listen.' He sang again, and although he sang alone, he heard two voices. He stopped and said, 'Is it you, Misery, who are singing with me?' Misery answered, 'Aye, master, I am singing with you.' 'Well, Misery, let us walk together.' 'We shall, master. I will never desert you now.'

"The poor man reached home, and Misery asked him to go to the tavern with him. The peasant answered, 'I have no money.' 'Oh, foolish peasant! What do you need money for? I see you have a sheepskin, but of what use is it? Summer will be here soon, you will not need to wear it anyhow. Let us go to the tavern and sell the sheep-skin.' The peasant and Misery went to the tavern and drank away the sheepskin. On the following day Misery began to moan that his head ached from drinking, and he again called upon his master to drink some wine. 'I have no money,' said the peasant. 'What do we need money for? Take your sledge and cart—those will do.'

"There was nothing to be done. The peasant could not rid himself of Misery. So he took his sledge and cart, dragged them to the tavern, and drank them away with his companion. The following morning Misery moaned even more and called upon his master to go drinking again; the peasant drank away his harrow and plow. Before a month had gone by, he had squandered everything; he had even pawned his hut to a neighbor and taken the money to a tavern. But Misery again pressed him: 'Come, let us go to the tavern.' 'No, Misery, do as you like, but as for me, I have nothing more to pawn or sell.' 'Why, has not your wife got two dresses? Leave her one, and the second we will drink away.' The peasant took one dress, drank it away, and thought: 'Now I am cleaned out! I have neither house nor home, nothing is left to me or my wife.'

"Next morning Misery awoke, saw that the peasant had nothing left to be taken away, and said: 'Master!' 'What is it, Misery?' 'Listen to me. Go to your neighbor and ask him for his cart and oxen.' The peasant thought and thought, and finally he said, 'Misery, if I drink away my neighbor's cart and oxen, he will shoot me.' 'Well, I do not ask that of you yet,' said Misery. 'Let us haul logs and earn some money for our drink.' The peasant went to his neighbor and said: 'Give me your cart and a pair of oxen for a while; I will work a week

to pay you for the hire of them.' 'What do you need them for?' 'To go to the woods for some logs.' The neighbor frowned and did not like it, for the man had a name for drinking at the tavern, but he was kind and said, 'Very well, take them; but don't overload the cart.' 'Of course I won't, my benefactor!' He brought the pair of oxen, sat with Misery on the cart, and drove toward the woods. On the way he found a log that was lying beside a field and had lain there many years, and he stopped the oxen and got down to try to put the log in the cart. Misery slipped away into some bushes for a moment, for he needed to take a piss, and the peasant had to tug at the heavy old log all alone. When he lifted it, lo and behold he saw a ditch that was filled to the brim with gold. 'Well, why do you stare?' cried Misery, who had now returned. 'Hurry up and get it in the cart.'

"The peasant set to work and filled the cart with gold. He took everything out of the ditch, down to the last kopek; when he saw that nothing at all was left, he said, 'Have a look, Misery. Is there any money left?' Misery leaned over the ditch. 'I don't see any more,' he said. 'Something's shining over there in the corner—see?' said the peasant. 'No, I don't see it.' 'Crawl into the ditch then, Misery; you'll see it.' Misery crawled into the ditch. He no sooner had got in than the peasant covered him with the log, which was heavy as an ox. 'It's better that you stay here,' said the peasant, 'for if I take you with me, you will make me drink away this fortune.' The peasant came home, stored the money in his cellar, took the oxen and cart back to his neighbor, and began to consider how to establish himself in society. He bought wood, built himself a large wooden house, and lived twice as richly as his brother.

"After some time, a long time or a short time, he went to the town to invite his brother and sister-in-law to his birthday celebration. 'What an idea!' his rich brother said to him. 'You have nothing to eat, yet you are celebrating your birthday!' and he laughed with scorn. 'True,' said the brother who had once been poor, 'at one time I had nothing to eat, but now, thank God, I am no worse off than you. Come and you will see.' 'Very well then, I will come.' The next day the rich brother and his wife came to the birthday feast; and lo and behold, the once wretched man had a large wooden house, new and lofty, such as not even his brother had. The peasant gave them a royal feast, fed them with all kinds of viands, and set various meads and wines before them, feeding his brother and sister-in-law first of all. The rich brother asked him: 'Tell me, please, how did you become so wealthy?' The peasant told him truthfully how miserable Misery had attached himself to him, how he had led him to drink away all his possessions, down to the last thread, till nothing was left but the soul in his body, and how one day Misery had left him for a moment, and how he had found the vast treasure and penned up Misery.

"The rich man was envious and angry. He thought to himself: 'I will go to the field, lift the log, and let Misery out—let him ruin my brother completely, so that he will never again dare boast of his riches to me.' He sent his wife home and rushed to the field. He drove to the big log, turned it over, and stooped to see what was beneath it. Before he could bend his head all the way down, Misery jumped out and sat on his neck. 'Ah,' he shrieked, 'you wanted to starve me to death in there, but I'll never leave you now.' 'Listen, Misery,' said the merchant, 'in truth it was not I who imprisoned you beneath that log.' 'Who did it then, if not you?' 'It was my brother who imprisoned you, and I came for the express purpose of freeing you again.' 'No, you are lying! You cheated me once, but you won't cheat me again.' Misery sat securely on the rich man's neck; the rich man carried him home, and his fortune began to dwindle. From early morning Misery applied himself to his task; every day he called upon the merchant to drink, and much of his wealth went to the tavern keeper. 'This is no way to live,' groaned the merchant. 'It seems to me that I have suffered sufficiently to pay for my selfishness and pride. It is high time I separated from Misery—but how?'

"He thought and thought and finally said to his wife, 'I will go and ask my brother for help.' 'Go then, fool,' said his wife, 'but your brother is an ape and a dolt and will not help you,' and she spit out the window. He came to his brother's house and said, 'Ah, my own brother, help me a little in my misery. I have behaved toward you like a pig, like a spider and a weasel and an eel, and like a carp, because I thought you were a foolish oaf and beneath my notice. But now I am chastised and brought to my senses, for Misery sits here on my neck both night and day, and I cannot shake him.'

" 'Brother, leave it to me,' said the brother who had been poor before, 'I will see to it.' He went out into his courtyard, cleft two oaken spikes, took a new wheel, and drove a spike into one end of the hollow shaft that went through the hub of the wheel. Then he came back to his brother who had Misery on his neck and said, 'Misery, why do you do nothing but ride on people's necks like a lummox?' 'What else shall I do?' asked Misery. 'What else? Come into the courtyard and play hide-and-seek.' Misery was delighted with this idea. They went into the yard. First the merchant brother hid and then the once-poor brother. Misery found both of them with ease, and now it was Misery's turn to hide. 'Well,' he said, 'you won't find me so soon. I can get into any hole, no matter how small!' 'Braggart,' said the once-poor brother. 'You can't even get into that wheel, let alone a hole.' 'I can't get into that wheel? Just wait and see how I slip into that wheel!' Misery crawled into the hollow shaft; the once-poor brother drove the second spike into the hollow shaft, picked up the wheel, and cast it, together with Misery, into the river. Misery drowned, and the brothers at last became steadfast friends, generous and loyal to one another to the death, and as rich as kings."

*hat*," said Chudu the Goat's Son, with a look of disgust, "is not how things happen!"

"Never mind," said the babe with a wink, "life follows art."

They traveled for a day, and for another and another, a short way or a long, and they came to the palace at last with their wagonloads of treasure. There was a great celebration, and Christopher the Sullen and Armida the Blacksmith's Daughter were married, and when the old king, many years later, was buried, Prince Christopher became king and made Chudu the Goat's Son (though he never learned his name) Prime Minister, and the babe Archbishop. Christopher the Sullen was considered on all sides to be the bravest, manliest, most quick witted of kings, and his queen the sweetest and most lovable of aristocratic ladies, though she secretly went off on long trips and fought dragons. The Prime Minister frightened off all enemies by his calculated rages and crafty, saw-toothed smiles; the Archbishop did miracles and grew famous for his sermons and moralizing tales; and the world rolled on.